THE ART OF
WORDSWORTH

THE ART OF
WORDSWORTH

»»» ☻ «««

Lascelles Abercrombie

ARCHON BOOKS

HAMDEN, CONNECTICUT

1965

First published 1952

Reprinted by permission of
Oxford University Press
in an unaltered and unabridged edition

Library of Congress Catalog Card Number: 65-14188
Printed in the United States of America

PREFATORY NOTE

THESE five lectures were delivered as a course on the Percy Turnbull Foundation at the Johns Hopkins University, in April 1935; they have never been published before in any form. The course was adapted and elaborated from an earlier series, given in 1931 at the University of Belfast; it also included a certain amount of material from a separate lecture on *Peter Bell*, the date and occasion of which I have been unable to discover. For the purpose of this book it was decided that the *Peter Bell* lecture should stand by itself, as an appropriate appendix to the main series; in order to avoid repetition I have accordingly made some adjustment to the text of both. Except for this, my editing has been confined to minor points of detail—chiefly where the printed page seemed to call for more formality than was presented by the colloquial structure and syntax of the original. Quotations have been checked and some references provided.

That my father did not himself prepare the lectures for publication before his death in 1938 was not, I am sure, due to any feeling of dissatisfaction with what he had written. It may be that he intended to do so, and that illness and the pressure of more immediate work prevented him. But I think it more likely that he wished to make use of the material, at some future time, in an extended treatment of Wordsworth's poetry: it was a subject that, for the last ten years of his life, had increasingly occupied his mind. More than once he spoke of such a project; I have no doubt that, had he lived, he would have realized this critical ambition.

I am grateful to the Oxford University Press for advice, and patience. To the late R. C. Trevelyan a particular debt is owing; it was he who first extracted the manuscript from my father's papers and set it in order, and he constantly interested himself in getting it into print. Without his exertions its publication would have been delayed even longer.

RALPH ABERCROMBIE

CONTENTS

I. INTRODUCTORY

M Y subject is the *art* of Wordsworth; and I dare
say, to some ears, this may sound a little odd. There
is still something rather paradoxical about his reputation. Everyone accepts him nowadays as one of our
greatest poets. The controversy which his poetry
provoked during his lifetime, and which went on
throughout the nineteenth century, has died away
by now. There seems nothing extravagant now in
the claim made by some of his admirers from the
first, and so powerfully reinforced by Matthew
Arnold, that he stands along with Shakespeare and
Milton as the third of the supremely great English
poets; and not merely that his eminence is of a
height comparable with theirs, but that it is of a kind
entirely distinct and peculiar to himself. Nevertheless, a relic of the old controversy persists. Many
critics have pointed out the careful deliberation with
which Wordsworth composed; witness the way he
continually altered his text (and on the whole,
though there are notable exceptions, improved it).
These critics may convince their readers; but their
readers, I am afraid, do not form a very large fraction
of the general public. And there the notion still is, it

seems, that this great and original poet *wanted art*. When he is at his best, he is praised for it: he did not need such factitious assistance. When he is at his worst, he is laught at for it: he was too obtuse to see its advantages. How, without art, he managed to be a poet at all, we are not told; but we must not expect the notions of the general public to form any exact theory. It is no doubt true that a person may say remarkable things without saying them very well; it is equally true that such things can never be mistaken for poetry.

This common paradoxical opinion, that Wordsworth was a great poet, but not a great *artist* in poetry, is plainly one of the things that a lecturer on the art of Wordsworth must face, and explain if he can. And the explanation must surely be, that in his art there is something decidedly unusual. It would indeed be very strange if it were true that Wordsworth, of all poets, was deficient in art. For it is not simply that what he did as a poet has imprest itself at large on the mind of the English-speaking peoples. He schooled his ambition by patient and lifelong study of the poets whom he regarded as the four great masters of the art in English—Chaucer, Spenser, Shakespeare, and Milton. He probably had a better knowledge of English poetry as a whole than anyone else of his time: and he thought about the nature and methods of poetry more deeply, more consistently, and more originally than anyone else in our literature, with the possible exception of Milton. And yet it is true that we seldom talk of the art of Wordsworth, analysing it and examining it piecemeal, as we so easily do of the art of Milton or Chaucer, of Coleridge or Tennyson, of Spenser or Pope. We seem content, as a rule, to account for his greatness by his thought or imagery (especially, of course, by his imagery of what we call *nature*), by his powers as a moralist or consoler, revealer or reconciler.

Does not this, then, simply mean that his greatness consists in his *matter*? That will hardly do, unless by *matter* we mean the same thing as *art*. For how is a poet to affect us by his matter? Only as he has made it effective on us by his art! He may have in his mind the most remarkable matter in the world; that is no good to us so long as it is simply in *his* mind. What concerns us is that this matter, and its power and its value, should be transported from his mind into ours; and that is what his art must do. To receive his matter is the same thing as to receive his art. Once we have received it, we can no doubt distinguish—to some extent, at any rate—what the poet says from the way he says it. Then we are in a different state of mind; we are criticizing what we have experienced. But we must have had the experience first, and to say that Wordsworth gives us this by his matter is only another way of saying that he gives it to us by his art.

These somewhat elementary considerations have here a special importance, for they are specially apt to be forgotten in Wordsworth's case. And we must take them a little further. When we have distinguisht the *way* a poet says what he has to say, we speak of distinguishing his technique from his matter. But a poet's art is not merely his technique. This *matter* of his we talk about—what is it? It is not brute stuff, conveyed by the technique like the load on a truck. It is not so much *carried* by the technique as *embodied* in it, as inextricably as vitality is in flesh. It is, in fact, living and purposive. It has a design on us, an intelligent design; it enters into our minds charged with a will of its own, and at once proceeds to exert it. This it does by no mechanical or calculable laws. It is a piece of the poet's mind transported into ours, a moment of his experience to which we have submitted, and which happens over again in us. Experience, however, never quite repeats itself. Like everything that is truly alive, this matter of the poet's has the property of adapting itself to its place: it becomes our experience while not ceasing to be his. All this could not happen unless the living particle of experience had become, so to speak, detachable from the poet's mind, with an individuality of its own. It has been shaped, ordered, isolated, organized, designed; above all, so unified in its own distinctive character that it will always be substantially the same experience whatever mind it may lodge in. This is the poet's matter; and its establishment or creation in the poet's own mind is the first stage in the composition of a poem. Whether it be simple or complex, whether it come about consciously and deliberately, or instinctively and spontaneously, or by a mixture of both, this process belongs as much to the art of a poem as the next stage does, its expression in language.

This first stage in the composition of a poem is naturally the one which most provokes our curiosity; unfortunately it is just the one about which we can find out the least. The poets themselves know little about it, but those of them who, like Wordsworth, are profoundly aware of themselves as poets, have no doubt of its supreme importance. It may complete itself with amazing rapidity, so that its elaboration and reverberation of an event may seem an almost instantaneous reaction. There are a good many cases of this in Wordsworth's poetry. Sara Hutchinson calls to him out of the window one evening to look at 'yon star', which 'has the sky all to itself'. He looks: 'O most ambitious Star!'—and instantly the star is himself, his soul, 'an Apparition in the place':

> And, while I gazed, there came to me a thought
> That I might step beyond my natural race
> As thou seem'st now to do.

Finely said, though, perhaps, a shade too discursive. We note that the poem evidently began as a sonnet; its impulse did not manage to concentrate itself sufficiently to fit into that most exacting form. It would have been a better poem if it had.

Sometimes Wordsworth's *extempore* poetry can be very splendid; witness the famous *Extempore Effusion upon the Death of James Hogg*. What a wealth of thought and imagination associated itself, in a moment, with the news of the Ettrick Shepherd's death! It gave us one of his finest lines—'Our haughty life is crowned with darkness'—and certainly one of his finest stanzas:

> Like clouds that rake the mountain-summits,
> Or waves that own no curbing hand,
> How fast has brother followed brother
> From sunshine to the sunless land!

Doubtless his mind was charged with memories, instantly responding to the event: Walter Scott, Coleridge, 'the heaven-eyed creature', Charles Lamb, Crabbe, Felicia Hemans. But how proportionably, as well as vividly, they enter into the simple and stately design of the whole poem—an instantaneous design!

This, however, was not characteristic of Wordsworth's genius. Very far from it; much the greatest part of his best work is the result of experience long incubated in the depth of his mind. What happened to it down there, who shall say? But we may be pretty sure, putting it in general terms, that it not only gradually settled into order and shapeliness, securing the subtle articulation of its parts, but enricht itself with association and feeling, and insisted on delighted perception of its significance. And this at last demanded utterance, sometimes with a demoniac, sometimes with a sort of elfin power. In a famous passage in the epilogue to that charming poem, *The Waggoner*, Wordsworth tells how he would sometimes be startled by the power over him of this store of old experiences in his mind. He generalizes this power as something uncanny, something not himself:

> Nor is it I who play the part,
> But a shy spirit in my heart,
> That comes and goes—will sometimes leap
> From hiding-places ten years deep;
> Or haunts me with familiar face,
> Returning, like a ghost unlaid,
> Until the debt I owe be paid.

In this connexion, we naturally recall that celebrated and pregnant remark of his that poetry 'takes its origin from emotion recollected in tranquillity'. The exact force intended by the phrase is not always clear when it is quoted out of its context. It is commonly taken as defining what Wordsworth thought poetry *ought* to be, and, remembering the defiant mood in which the Preface of 1800 was written, perhaps it does; but only because it recorded the *fact* that in his case actually occurred. That was how poetry took its origin in him; and, in 1800, that perhaps was quite enough to make him mean, thus poetry *ought* to originate. We had better quote the whole passage:

Poetry is the spontaneous overflow of powerful feelings: it takes its origin from emotion recollected in tranquillity; the emotion is contemplated till, by a species of reaction, the tranquillity gradually disappears, and an emotion, kindred to that which was before the subject of contemplation, is gradually produced, and does itself actually exist in the mind. In this mood successful composition generally begins, and in a mood similar to this it is carried on.

Thus it appears that by recollecting emotion in tranquillity, a secondary and similar emotion is induced, and this overflows as poetry. What is gained by this delayed and secondary action? Why must the composition of poetry be thus postponed? Why is the poet to refrain from his first emotion and wait till

he can induce a subsequent and similar emotion?
Wordsworth knew very well why. It is because of
what happens in the depth of the poet's mind while
the emotion (or, to use a larger term, the *experience*)
is lying stored away there—as mysteriously active
within itself as a germinating seed, and, like the
buried seed, obscurely nourisht by that which hides
it. What happens down there is in fact, as I have
said, the first stage in the composition of a poem,
whether the time it takes be long or short. And it is
characteristic of Wordsworth that as a rule it took
a long time; sometimes a very long time indeed, a
matter of many years. The necessity for this, I think,
we may easily—I will not say understand, but at any
rate believe—if we reflect on the nature of Wordsworth's finest and greatest work. That, however, is
what I must try to elucidate. But even a poem which
seems such an immediate reply to the challenge of
a moment as *Stepping Westward* only issued into
verbal form after its experience had slept silently in
his mind for more than a year. We may guess that
is why, when the time came for *words*, it did at last
become the perfect thing it is—a delicate and lucid
suggestion of an unaccountable enchantment:

> The dewy ground was dark and cold;
> Behind, all gloomy to behold;
> And stepping westward seemed to be

> A kind of *heavenly* destiny:
> I liked the greeting; 'twas a sound
> Of something without place or bound;
> And seemed to give me spiritual right
> To travel through that region bright.

What conscious process could transform the casual question—'*What, you are stepping westward?*'—into a spell which could bestow *spiritual right* to travel through that region bright?

The capital instance, however, is *The Prelude*. There, the grandest, the subtlest, the most exalted of his experiences became by long incubation not only transparently intelligible in their extraordinary significance: the whole process of psychological development in which they occur had thereby also become, without requiring any of the usual arts of narrative, an astonishingly interesting and beautifully articulated story. *The Prelude* is thus typical of the art of Wordsworth. And it is typical of the man. It not only tells us of these remarkable experiences, it tells us also how he became capable of them; and to this he was continually looking back. Over and over again, in the poetry that we value most in him, the glory of the past shines upon the present and transfigures it. To a quite remarkable degree, past experience in him was living energy, either interpreting the present, or dividing his attention between the senses' immediate delight and 'the Mind's internal heaven':

> some happy tone
> Of meditation slipping in between
> The beauty coming and the beauty gone.

Let me return now to the question of what we really mean by the poet's *matter*. I simplified it by speaking of a particle or moment of his experience. That would give us lyrical poetry, but a poet's matter may equally well consist of a system of such particles or moments—a system which would itself be a distinct unity of several related experiences: and this will account for narrative or reflective or dramatic poetry. Also, for the sake of emphasis, I put it rather too metaphorically when I spoke of the poet's experience being transported from his mind into ours. Strictly, of course, that does not and cannot happen. Experience is always an absolutely private possession; no one can part with it. It is we ourselves who must provide the matter of a poem, not the poet. The fact that there is such a thing as the art of poetry depends on our ability to respond in imagination to the stimulus of words. It is thus that we respond, so far as we are capable of responding, to the whole technique of a poet's language: it excites an imaginative experience in us, which at the same time it controls. But that technique has been constructed by the poet as an exact equivalent of his own experience, an equivalent in terms of the power he understands in words: and the power of words being more or less predictable, the experience provoked in our minds will be an *imitation* of the poet's experience. Behind everything, then, that may properly be called technique in the poet's art, there is always this actuating and moulding force, and it will only inspire the technique to be efficient on our minds according as it is itself efficient on the technique; shaping, unifying, designing, just as it has itself been shaped, unified, designed. Inspiration is, indeed, the best name for this force—for what is commonly called the poet's matter. It is true that the word *inspiration* is sometimes used, like the word *matter*, in a sense that puts it apart from, even in contrast with, what we mean by art. I am not concerned with that sense whether it refers to supernatural energy or to confused psychology. What I mean by inspiration belongs by its very nature to the art of the poet.

But *art* is a notoriously shifty and uncertain word. When we are discussing some particular branch of art, or the art of some particular person, it would seem quite natural to use the word in the special sense which limits it to the artist's technique. Thus 'the art of Milton' might very well be expected to refer to his rhythms, his vowels and consonants, his imagery, the structure of his sentences, and so on; it might not be necessary to do more than allude incidentally to the energy behind it all, to Milton's inspiration. In any poetry whatever, there are certain aspects of the technique which can always be thus isolated. Prosody is the obvious instance. We can speak of Milton's prosody and compare it with Shakespeare's or Wordsworth's without raising any question at all of Milton's puritanism or Shakespeare's humanity or Wordsworth's pantheism. This kind of discussion would be still more likely in arts like painting or music, where you have a clearly distinguishable science or discipline of technique, forming a study in itself. The mere use of such technique is enough to supply plenty of topics for debate. We can easily talk of draughtsmanship and colour and design, of harmony and orchestration and melodic development, without necessarily concerning ourselves very much with what the painter or composer *means* by it all.

Yet, of course, this procedure is always an abstraction from the art as a whole. The technique is what it is because of the inspiration which is in it. And in poetry, this abstraction may be a good deal more arbitrary than in the other arts; there will be cases in which, outside certain strictly limited aspects, it will prove very precarious, even quite unworkable. A poet's art consists just as much in the way he manages the meaning of his words as in the way he manages the rhythm of his syllables. And as soon as we touch the meaning of his words, we touch what he has to say, his matter, his inspiration. Nevertheless, with most poets, we can still hold off from that in discussing the mere elaboration of their use of the meaning of words. How much there is to say about imagery and metaphor and epithets in Spenser, for example, or in Keats or Tennyson! But not in Wordsworth; and so definitely and noticeably not in him, that his case cannot but present itself as something exceptional. There is not a great deal to say about those phonetic aspects of his art which do not directly involve intellectual meaning—metre and cadence and syllabic sound; and as soon as we leave these, it is scarcely possible to draw even an arbitrary boundary which will distinguish what he has to say from the way he says it—as we commonly put it, his matter from his art.

This, I think, is what is really meant by Wordsworth's 'simplicity'. This at any rate, I am sure, is why the world has seemed reluctant to allow him *art*. His poetry will not submit in any satisfactory manner to that process of abstraction by which we usually arrive at what we call a poet's art. That does not mean there is little to say about the way he manages language. There is plenty to say about that; but you cannot talk about Wordsworth's technique without at once bringing in—what I should call his inspiration, but what is commonly, and sometimes rather disastrously, called his matter. The power of his poetry is thus supposed to depend on his matter; and the ambiguity that word conceals suggests that it therefore depends on something which is not art: which lands us in the paradox I spoke of at the beginning. I should not object to the statement that his power depends on his inspiration. That might seem a truism which applies to all poets; to Wordsworth it applies in a very special manner. And by inspiration I do not mean something outside his art; to allege this as the source of his poetic greatness is not to absolve us in any way from treating him as an artist, however extraordinary his 'matter' may be in its moral or philosophical value, in its power of consoling or reconciling or revealing.

Here is some indication of the peculiar sort of greatness which may be attributed to Wordsworth in the succession of the English poets, and it should become clearer in the course of this discussion. Meanwhile, a very pertinent reflection has, I have no doubt, occurred to you, which it would be folly not to notice. I daresay it will have already appeared that I am what is called a Wordsworthian. I will not deny it: I am. Crabb Robinson, that faithful friend, said, in 1815: 'Wordsworth, in answer to the common reproach that his sensibility is excited by objects which produce no effect on others, admits the fact, and is proud of it.' The remark exactly fits the sect to which I belong. We Wordsworthians, too, are excited by objects which produce no effect on others; we too are proud of it. But surely, it will be asked, even a Wordsworthian must admit that the notion of Wordsworth's deficiency in art receives the strongest possible encouragement from Wordsworth himself. How can you call an artist the man who was capable of writing, in his description of a country church,

> Admonitory texts inscribed the walls,
> Each, in its ornamental scroll, enclosed . . .

and who has not heard of the spade of Mr. Wilkinson? Does not that implement owe its celebrity simply to bad art? Yes, Wordsworth could be not only no artist, but so positively a bad artist that his reputation to some considerable degree is affected by it. But is there any poet in the world whose art might not be queried by quoting him at his worst? We can say of Wordsworth that, perhaps, with him the ratio of failure to success is unusually high; the success he aimed at was, after all, unusually difficult.

Naturally, when I speak of the art of Wordsworth, I mean the Wordsworth that so greatly succeeded, not the Wordsworth that sometimes so lamentably failed.

This, however, would be to treat the objection too cavalierly. I think it is right to say that the assertion of Wordsworth's failure as an artist has somewhat changed its ground, since the days of his contemporary readers. To them his success as a poet seemed to be a matter of hit or miss; you could never be sure, since it seemed mere chance, whether he would come off or not. We do not look on him quite like that nowadays; that view was largely due to the fact that his art was unfamiliar. People used to laugh, remember, at *Alice Fell*; they found *We are Seven* merely childish. Such subjects as Wordsworth chose in poems like these are no longer shocking to us; the methods he used no longer seem deliberate and wanton defiance of tradition. We are still free to criticize, of course; but we can do so without being distracted by novelty from the truth of their pathos, their piercing insight, the restraint and tact of their workmanship. For myself, I should say that *Alice Fell* is a perfect little masterpiece, and *We are Seven* a poem of singularly profound meaning: and today there is nothing extraordinary in such judgements. We need not insist on them; it is simply that we should not think much of a critic nowadays who could not give these poems serious consideration as important works of art, whether he liked them or not. Even in the opening lines of *Goody Blake and Harry Gill*—

> Oh! what's the matter? What's the matter?
> What is't that ails young Harry Gill?
> That evermore his teeth they chatter,
> Chatter, chatter, chatter still!

we can see that what Wordsworth was trying to do was well worth doing, though just there he may not have been doing it very happily.

There is, then, a Wordsworth whom everyone nowadays accepts. His oddities may be displeasing; some of them may still seem ridiculous. But we can see now that they are as much the sign of his peculiar genius as his subtleties are; he would not be the poet he is without them. Whatever we may think of them, they are not due to incompetence. But there is another Wordsworth, one whom no one need—and, at his worst, whom no one can—accept. This is the Wordsworth who really did fail in the art of poetry. Note, however, that, though his work was often enough merely dull and flat, he did not fail for lack of technique. He was steept in the language of seventeenth and eighteenth century poetry, but either it did not fit what he had to say, or else its

elaboration took the place of saying anything worth
saying; and if there is anything worse than technique
misapplied, it is empty technique.

This is the later Wordsworth who gradually
emerges as the early Wordsworth gradually fades.
His failure in the art of poetry is thus a matter of
biography. I do not mean that his biography will
explain his failure. So far as we understand it at
present, it certainly does not, and perhaps it never
will. It is by no means clear that the history of the
man can explain the history of the poet, and in the
case of Wordsworth, the history of the man has not
yet been thoroughly mastered. The official life—the
Memoirs written by his nephew, the Bishop of Lin-
coln—though dull and not very understanding, is
still a useful performance; but it naturally stressed
the latter part of his life, when he had triumphed
over perhaps the most formidable opposition that
ever attempted to cry down a great poet, and had
become a national figure, his eminence everywhere
acknowledged. Some forty years afterwards came
one of the most beautiful essays in biography of
modern times—a work to which all Wordsworthians, and all lovers of English poetry, stand in debt
'still paying, still to owe': Émile Legouis's study of
the youth of Wordsworth. Ever since, it has been
clear where the emphasis must lie in any account

either of the poet or the man. Thus we find that when the full life of Wordsworth was at last written by Professor Harper[1] on an adequate scale, with immense and thoroughly reorganized information, Wordsworth's middle and old age were disposed of a good deal more rapidly, and less sympathetically, than the early years. Nevertheless, the later Wordsworth presents some extremely interesting problems, and to understand these would illuminate the nature of the whole man. The balance has been recently adjusted by Miss Edith Batho's important study[2] in which she shows how necessary it is to be fair to his mature years, and how strangely they have been misunderstood.

Certainly, Wordsworth's decreasing power as a poet goes along, roughly speaking, with certain well-known changes in the man. But between some of these changes and the decline of his genius a causal connexion has been too easily assumed. He has been reproacht for becoming respectable; there seems no real reason why a respectable man should not write good poetry. And in some cases the changes in his mind and behaviour have been formulated much too rigidly. He turned Tory; but the standard

[1] *William Wordsworth: His Life, Works and Influence*, George McLean Harper, Murray, 1916.
[2] *The Later Wordsworth*, Edith Batho, Constable, 1934.

of humanity was still not set for him by the rich and powerful, but by the poor and obscure; and in his attitude to poetry he was always the ardent Communist of his youth. What he told Sir George Beaumont early in the century was his opinion to the last: 'No liberal art aims merely at the gratification of an individual or class: the painter or poet is degraded in proportion as he does so.' He strongly approved of the principles of the Chartists, though disapproving of their methods. Indeed, politically speaking, he can never have been a very good Tory. Perhaps the best comment on his attitude to party politics is his remark to Daniel Stuart in 1809: 'If I have a hill to climb, and cannot do it without a walking stick, better have a dirty one than none at all.' The subject is too complicated for full discussion here, but it should be remembered that after his revulsion from the French Revolution he found his thoughts and feelings deeply engaged by another and quite different revolution—the Industrial Revolution. Here everything he had always valued and believed in called on him to be a counter-revolutionary. Only too clearly he foresaw the hideous evils which the Industrial Revolution was to produce; and the party that still supported the French Revolution was also the party that stood for exploiting country and people through industrial manufacture. That by itself might account for Wordsworth's siding with the Tories. *His* Toryism, at any rate, scarcely accounts for, though to some extent it accompanied, his poetic decline. A good deal more of the mind of his youth survived his political metamorphosis than is commonly supposed, and the traditional picture of the old man's narrow dogmatism, arrogance, and egotism is mere caricature. And though in the poem called *Steamboats, Viaducts and Railways*, he saw

> Motions and means, on land and sea at war
> With old poetic feeling . . .

it was not without perceiving some compensation. He was even capable of new poetic feeling for such things; he told Gladstone that the form of the steamboat was 'rather poetical than otherwise to the eye'.

But there is one change which may safely be taken as the sign at least of his poetic decline. It is often supposed that when he became, inwardly and outwardly, a Church of England man, he thereby repudiated the unorthodoxy of his youth. It may be debated whether there need have been any hostility between Church of England doctrine and what is commonly called the pantheism of his youth. Nevertheless, it seems certain that when he did submit to

Anglicanism, that kind of experience—for it was never a formulated doctrine—which we rather crudely but conveniently call his pantheism had died away in him. There is, indeed, right to the very end, much in his later work that reminds us how exquisitely and subtly he would still see nature, and tells us of his pure aesthetic delight in it. It was in his old age that he noted how the ash trees of *Airey-Force Valley* made in the stirring of the breeze

> A soft eye-music of slow-waving boughs . . .

and how the lambs in the spring sunlight

> Gambol—each with his shadow at his side
> Varying its shape wherever he may run . . .

with the same eyes that long ago had seen with youthful glee the running hare raise from the plashy earth the mist

> that, glittering in the sun,
> Runs with her all the way wherever she doth run.

The same eyes, but not the same mind! Now, when his eyes rejoice in *The Primrose of the Rock*, it is a theological reflection that can make 'each soul a separate heaven, A court for Deity'. Once, the primrose itself could have done that—

> There was a time when meadow, grove, and stream,
> The earth, and every common sight,
> To me did seem
> Apparelled in celestial light . . .

Now, instead of that actual experience of glory, transfiguring earth, *moral resolve* (certainly a noble one) asserts itself, and it is by a metaphor that

> Trust in that sovereign law can spread
> New glory o'er the mountain's head,
>   Fresh beauty through the vale.[1]

Nature, to the later Wordsworth, is indeed his best encouragement and dearest consolation as well as an unfailing aesthetic delight. So it has been to many other poets, both before and after him, though few have had Wordsworth's intimacy and nicety of observation. Not very different from the later Wordsworth's *sentiment for nature* is what we find, for instance, in Count Xavier de Maistre:-'Often', he says, 'the aspect of nature comforts me; I have an affection for the rocks and the trees, and it seems as if God had given me his creatures for my friends.' In one of his very last poems—and it is one of the tenderest and loveliest he ever wrote—Wordsworth permits himself wistfully to speculate on the joy it would be if nature could *know* what a friend she is:

> So fair, so sweet, withal so sensitive,
> Would that the little Flowers were born to live,
> Conscious of half the pleasure which they give;
>
> That to this mountain-daisy's self were known
> The beauty of its star-shaped shadow, thrown
> On the smooth surface of this naked stone!

[1] 'The Wishing-Gate Destroyed', ll. 58–60.

But he rebukes himself for these 'fond fancies': nature must be enjoyed as what she is, 'All vain desires, all lawless wishes quelled'. Once these were very far from lawless wishes, vain desires, fond fancies. Once to enjoy nature as what she is imposed no limits to speculation, for nature knows no limits; to contemplate nature then was to enter into the divine community of all being, to be aware of the infinite *in* things and transcending things. That was gone. The grandeur and delicacy and absolute individuality of his youthful experience no longer lived in the depth of his mind, with the power to emerge and create in language the perfect image of itself.

Wordsworth's failure as a great poet lay in that first stage in poetic composition, the formation of the energy of inspiration. He came to fail in that because the energy itself failed. Why, we can only guess; when, we are still debating. Perhaps the great Immortality Ode, the climax of his art, marks the turning-point in his psychological history. The difficulty is that there is so much excellence scattered throughout the long tract of his decline. You turn over the pages of some edition arranged in chronological order (entirely against his own strong wishes, by the way) and you think you have at last come to the end of the Wordsworth that matters. You turn a page or two more, and there, in the

wilderness, you come on something which the greatest poet, the most scrupulous artist, might envy.
Sometimes it may be what seems like an echo of the
earlier magic, as when he imagines old age remembering the turbulent delights of youth and bids it

> steal to his allotted nook
> Contented and serene;
>
> With heart as calm as lakes that sleep,
> In frosty moonlight glistening;
> Or mountain rivers, where they creep
> Along a channel smooth and deep,
> To their own far-off murmurs listening.[1]

Sometimes, out of the profoundly changed habit of
his mind new inspiration arises, with shaping power
comparable to the old, as in the *Vernal Ode*, or in the
last of the River Duddon Sonnets:

Still glides the Stream, and shall for ever glide;
The Form remains, the Function never dies,
While we, the brave, the mighty, and the wise,
We Men, who in our morn of youth defied
The elements, must vanish;—be it so!
Enough, if something from our hands have power
To live, and act, and serve the future hour;
And if, as toward the silent tomb we go,
Through love, through hope, and faith's transcendent
    dower,
We feel that we are greater than we know.

Indeed, several of his finest sonnets belong to the

[1] 'Memory', ll. 23–29 (1823).

later years: 'Scorn not the sonnet', *Mutability*, 'Tax not the Royal Saint'. And with what swift and vivid activity poetic impulse could work in his old age, the *Extempore Effusion upon the Death of James Hogg* has already reminded us. But when all is said, after, say, 1816, the poet whose greatness challenges the very greatest, who can give us something the like of which we can get nowhere else—that poet is dying or dead. It is with that poet we shall be mainly concerned in this discussion; and later, perhaps, we may feel we can hazard a guess why the inspiration which made him what he was at length failed him.

II. INSPIRATION

THEY say that mathematicians build their imposing structures on foundations which the philosophers regard with apprehension. So it is with criticism. We cannot go far without making distinctions, and of some of them philosophy is very suspicious; particularly of the one which criticism finds the most useful of all, the distinction between what a poet says and the way he says it. In the first place, says philosophy, the distinction cannot be made, for it is impossible to tell where one ends and the other begins. In the second place it ought not to be made. The dichotomy is not only unworkable, it is false; for the intention to say a thing consists in saying it. Now that may be true metaphysically, or it may be true of ordinary speech. But poetry is not the same thing as ordinary speech, and it is at any rate true enough that a poet has something in his mind first, and then proceeds to say it. He may have it in his mind for years without saying it and then labour for years in order to say it; all the time it remains there, unsaid or incompletely said, but insisting on being said eventually. This does not mean, of course, that he has the poem in his head; the poem does not exist until the

impulse towards it in the poet's mind has been perfectly translated into its verbal equivalent, and in
that process many things must emerge—especially
in the detail of his art—of which he could not have
been aware or could not, properly speaking, have
intended until he actually said them. In that sense,
the intention of the poem *is* the poem itself. Nevertheless, I shall assume that it is true enough for the
practical purposes of criticism—and I believe there
is a sense in which it is really true—to speak of the
impulse to compose a poem as preceding the elaborately designed system of language which it produces.

As for this distinction being unworkable, that
would be true if it were proposed to draw any precise
boundary between the two. But there is no need for
that; the intelligent critic should be fully aware,
firstly, that the distinction must be a very broad one,
and secondly, that it is only made at all, by abstraction, to enable criticism to manage its affairs conveniently. It is only when we pass from pure aesthetic
experience to analysis that any such distinction
occurs to us. The poet's elaborately designed system
of language is what we call his technique; a system
composed of all the power which language can exert
on our minds, by its sound and by its meaning, designed to one ultimate end. We distinguish this from
his *matter*, or what I would rather call his *inspiration*;

from that which has been committed to it or from that which is received from it, according as we take the poet's or the reader's point of view.

There are really two propositions here. First, that it is generally possible to give separate discussion to technique and to inspiration. Secondly, that inspiration is prior to technique. Now you may remember that I pointed out how exceedingly difficult it is in the case of Wordsworth to make the usual distinction between what he says and the way he says it, simply because the nature of his technique is so closely and exactly conditioned by the nature of his inspiration. It is just because we can generally assume the distinction to be possible, that the case of Wordsworth is so remarkable. But this does not touch our second proposition. Though we cannot discuss his technique without bringing in his inspiration, the fact that we can think of his inspiration as the condition governing his technique means that we can think of it as preceding his technique. We can think of it as an impulse to compose poetry, and talk about its peculiar nature as such an impulse.

I gave you some reasons why it seems to me better to speak of a poet's *inspiration* rather than of his *matter*. There is another reason, a cogent one. When we talk of a poet's matter, we are apt to leave out the question of his *motive* in dealing with such

matter; and this may be a question of capital importance. The word *inspiration*, however, evidently
includes motive; so that when we say the art of
Wordsworth's poetry cannot be discussed (as the
art of so many poets can) without bringing in its
inspiration, one of the things we mean is that it cannot be discussed without considering what its motive
was. This, judging by other poets, might seem to
confront us with a very familiar difficulty in criticism.
Actually, Wordsworth's case is such that he is the
ideal subject for the ideal critical method. That
method would follow the same order as the poet's
composition: it would begin with what the poet intended to say, and go on from this to consider what
he actually did say, and how he said it. Now in most
instances *what* the poet says is, or used to be, clear
enough, allowing for the inevitable differences in the
way we respond to his technique. But those differences become much more serious when we ask ourselves what his *motive* was—what he *meant* by saying
what he did say. The difficulty is not confined to
poetic criticism. I recently saw in an exhibition in
Paris a charming picture by the seventeenth-century
painter, Georges de Latour: a cottage interior lit by
a candle, with an old man asleep in a chair, and a
buxom young woman standing over him and gently
waking him up. Two descriptive titles of that picture

were offered; one was, *An old man asleep being roused by a girl*; the other, *The angel appearing to Saint Joseph*. You will agree that there is a considerable difference in the attributed motives here. Either would be possible in Latour's time; who shall say which is the right one? And it is just as much a problem, what Shakespeare meant by *Hamlet* or Virgil by the *Aeneid*, as what Beethoven meant by the C minor symphony, or Michelangelo by the statue called *Dawn*. Everyone is imprest by the Witches in *Macbeth*, but no one knows quite what they mean.

This difficulty does not seem to have been perceived by Manzoni, who, in the famous preface to *Il Conte di Carmagnola* (that noble poem), laid down once and for all the principles of what I have called the ideal method of criticism. Every poem, says Manzoni, in his trenchant way, contains within itself the principles by which it should be judged. They may be summed up in three questions: What was the author's intention? Was it a worthy intention? Has the author carried it out? This is admirable; but how are we to know what the author's intention was? For it is not in this order that we take in his work. We first receive his technique, and from this we understand his matter; so far, there should be no difficulty. But as for what he *intends* by his matter, in the vast majority of cases all we have to go on is

the way we happen to be stirred by the devices he
employs to stir us; and who can be sure he has been
stirred as the poet intended? One critic reads the *Bac-
chae* and says: 'Here Euripides, after long scepticism,
turns at last to religion in deep reverence and ecstati-
cally exultant faith.' Another reads the play and says:
'Here the sceptical Euripides gives us his last and
most terrible indictment of the evils of religion.'
Would not both critics say, each equally firm in the
impression the poem has made on him, that the poet
has 'carried out his intention'? For in either case, the
only intention discoverable was the way the poet's
art affected the critic. This is an extreme example,
but something of the kind is always liable to happen
in poetic criticism, as in that of any art, when we
come to the question of *motive*.

That is why criticism is so ready to consult biography. If only we could understand the man, surely
we should be able to perceive the intention of his
art! Shall we not understand him, if we can see
how he lived in his own particular world? And how
can we be brought to see that more authoritatively
than in the facts of his life, how more objectively
than in the reports of his behaviour? Shall we not
thereby learn just what we want to know, his intellectual, emotional, and moral attitude to things—
everything that can give us the very spirit of his art?

Unfortunately, no: or only by pure guesswork. It is extraordinarily difficult to make out the real man in the facts of his life and his reported behaviour. And with a poet, what reason have we to suppose that the real man is any more apparent in what is called his life than in his poetry? His poetry is his life; outside his poetry, his visible behaviour may be largely unimportant for what we want to know, or quite misleading. In two recent studies of Wordsworth[1] the dangers and ineptitudes of biographical interpretation have been remarkably illustrated. The method there adopted seems, roughly, to have been this: a hasty glance at the facts—giving neither adequate acquaintance with them nor power to understand them—suggests what might have been the real man. This suggestion is taken as established; it is freely elaborated and vigorously coloured, and then appeal is made to the facts to justify it. The justification is by that kind of guesswork which is called psychology; and it is such enthusiastic guesswork that it infects the facts, and subdues them to what they ought to be.

Until a few years ago, except for his revolutionary youth (which, after all, was soon over), Wordsworth's outwardly placid and regular life told us

[1] *Wordsworth*, Herbert Read, Faber & Faber, 1930 (new edition, 1950). *The Lost Leader: A Study of Wordsworth*, Hugh I'Anson Fausset, Cape, 1933.

little about his art. Then it was found that this outwardly placid and regular life concealed a remarkable secret: he had had a passionate affair with a
lady in France who had borne him an illegitimate
daughter. Wordsworth's stock perceptibly rose, and
the psychological biographers got busy. Here at last
was the hidden cause of the profound passion of his
early poems; here, too, in the shame and remorse
that followed—in the long and cankering conceal-
ment of his sin—the hidden cause of his violent revulsion of feeling against the French Revolution.
This was why he came to hate France and all things
French, why he called Voltaire dull and said the
French had no literature. This explains his stubborn
and unamiable adherence to the Tories and the
Church of England, and, finally, the woeful decline
of his poetic powers.

It will not work. The facts do not fit, chronologically or otherwise. There is no evidence that Wordsworth ever did conceal his French mistress or his
French daughter,[1] though it seems to be taken as
a sign of guilty repression that he did not gossip
about them. We do not know how he looked back
on that grievous affair; but he was not a Victorian,
and the fact that he had a natural daughter certainly

[1] His wife and his sister knew the facts, and so did Crabb
Robinson and the Clarksons. See Edith Batho, *The Later Wordsworth*, 1933.

did not poison his life. As to his revulsion against the French Revolution, that was an experience which he had in common with thousands of Englishmen of his time; and it is not to be supposed that they all had illegitimate daughters in France. Wordsworth, and they, had something much more shocking than that to bear. It was bad enough that the stupid policy of England had fatally deflected the energies of the Revolution, though the consequent imminence of disaster was so terrible that most of them forgot that England had drawn it on herself. The really tragic thing was that the Revolution, the principles of which they had hailed with such exultation, had gone wrong not so much because of the wickedness or incompetence of human nature, as because of those very principles themselves. That is the thing to remember, not Annette Vallon, when we reflect on the change in Wordsworth's attitude to France. His connexion with Annette was an incident of mere passion in his life. The mind, the personality, the outlook, the politics of that strong-minded French-woman[1] were quite incompatible with his. Separation was inevitable—as inevitable, no doubt, as at first their merely passionate conjunction had been. The incident tells us as little about the peculiar passion

[1] See Émile Legouis, *William Wordsworth and Annette Vallon*, 1922.

of his early poems, as its prudent end and prosaic consequence tell us about the decline of his art.

Biography, as a guide to the real man, to the inmost mind and the deep foundations of experience in him, is as uncertain and may be as misleading with Wordsworth as with most other poets. But the remarkable thing about Wordsworth is that we do not need such a guide. His singular position consists in this, that we have, directly given *in* his art, the very information *about* his art which in most poets we can only obtain by inference, and seldom quite reliably. We have something much more certain than our own possibly temperamental response to his technique, something much more certain than mere biography, to tell us what sort of a mind he had, and what his personal world was like—that private world with which his mind, by its powers of creation and selection and interpretation, surrounded itself; what, in fact, his poetry intended. We have *The Prelude*; and *The Prelude* is not only the capital document in Wordsworthian criticism, it is also one of the greatest poems in the English language. Indeed, apart from dramatic poetry, I would reckon it as one of the three English poems that may truly be called grand—grand in scale, grand in subject, grand in execution.

How, then, does *The Prelude*, with its revelation

of the *man*, contribute to our understanding of Wordsworth's art? It is not primarily the function of the poet's art to give us himself but to give us significant experience; and our judgement of his success in doing this will be our judgement of the beauty of his art. It is because his experience is significant that the poet is urged to express it, and we are willing to receive it. Experience, however, cannot but be personal; and the more we feel of the poet's personality in the experience his art transmits to us, the better we understand the nature of the experience to which we submit, and the force of the significance it carries. For what do we mean by the poet's personality—that is, the personality we feel *in his art*? We mean that peculiarly individual relationship with his world, inner and outer, in which the spirit of the man most naturally and profoundly and completely lives. In this central habit of experience his poetry originates; out of this general source proceed those particular experiences which, when he has expressed them in words, we call his poems. This is that poetic personality we have in mind when we name Keats or Shelley, Herrick or Campion, Pope or Dryden; this inmost manner of experience is what makes a poet's art peculiarly his own, manifest in his style. It may be something quite different from anything his mere biography can show us. That is why

I call it his *poetic* personality—the serene and sane stability at the core of Tasso's crazy behaviour, the deep well of passion in the midst of Goethe's serenity. And it is precisely because his poetic experience proceeds out of this fundamental relationship between himself and his world that the poet's self-expression comes to us charged with significance. Its universal significance is this very harmony which has *formed* the manner of its existence—the profound harmony of a mind with its world.

To this central habit of the poet's experience, this essential spirit of the man as poet, all our intelligent delight in his art urges us, sooner or later, to penetrate. We always have the sense of it in his work, and by systematic study of the whole of his poetry we may form a strong, though perhaps not very definable, impression of it. By the conveyance of the several impressions made by a number of particular poems, we get some general impression of the poetic personality out of which they all emerge; and the stronger this general impression is, the more understanding our enjoyment of each poem will be. Thus, the man who knows all Shakespeare's plays will read any one of them with a finer and more perceptive enjoyment than the man whose reading of that play is his first experience of Shakespeare, or who knows only a few of the others. The mere mention of

Shakespeare is sufficient to remind us how far short of the ideal method of criticism this falls; so far short, that it is best to leave out of our criticism altogether any consideration of what Shakespeare *intended*. We can never know what Shakespeare meant to do; whereas what he actually did is certain: he produced this or that impression on us. Beyond this we cannot securely go; upon this sound criticism must be content to base itself; so it is with the vast majority of poets.

But the entirely characteristic thing about Wordsworth is that we *can* securely go beyond this. He wrote *The Prelude*; and the subject and the art of *The Prelude* combine to give us precisely that central habit of experience out of which all his poetry comes. In Wordsworth, as in no other poet, we can know at once the poetic personality and the significance it intends. In other poets we feel and try to understand that these are ultimately one and the same thing; in Wordsworth we not only know their identity, we know how and why they are the same. It is true that *The Prelude* is a work of art, and some variation in the way we respond to it is therefore inevitable. For our present purposes this is negligible. Its inspiration is Wordsworth's intention to reveal the formation and nature of that inmost habit of experience which made him the poet he was—that unique rela-

tionship between his mind and his world in which
he most deeply and vividly lived, and which con-
stitutes his poetic personality. The subject of *The
Prelude* is identical with its intention. If you grasp
the subject you thereby grasp its intention; and it is
not about a poem's subject that we are likely to be
uncertain. The case here is not, as it is in *Hamlet* or
Paradise Lost, the *Aeneid* or the *Divine Comedy*, of
a subject that is clear enough, while what the poet
intends by it can only be inferred, since all we can
know of it is our own interpretation of the subject.
In *The Prelude*, as in Lucretius' great poem, subject
and intention are all one.

The theme of the poem—*The Growth of a Poet's
Mind*—is exhibited in narrative form. It is much
more than autobiography, it is a story of universal
significance, of which Wordsworth's own unique
experience is offered as the type. It is the story of the
mind, greatly conscious of its own enigma, gradually
establishing its secure relationship with a world
equally enigmatic. The two enigmas indeed, remain;
but we understand that they are bound together in
one inevitable destiny of companionship. The nature
of each reflects the nature of the other. Each calls to
the other, and has its answer. This is the modern
epic; this is the heroic strain today, the grand theme
of man's latter experience; and grandly *The Prelude*,

its first enunciation, declares it. Like the *Iliad*, the *Aeneid*, the *Divine Comedy*, *Paradise Lost*—*The Prelude* inaugurates an epoch in poetry with 'things unattempted yet in prose or rhyme'. And like those other inaugural poems, it is not only conspicuous because it is the first to be so inspired, but because this very priority carries with it a sort of pioneering energy which shows itself in a new splendour of art.

Wordsworth is often called the poet of nature. He is the poet of many things besides; but it is in his relationship with nature that his poetic inspiration originates, and the history of this relationship is the subject of *The Prelude*. What sort of a relationship it came to be is suggested by the very first words of the poem:

> Oh there is blessing in this gentle breeze,
> A visitant that while it fans my cheek
> Doth seem half-conscious of the joy it brings
> From the green fields, and from yon azure sky.

Nothing could be more primitive in its matter than such a moment of experience as that—the sense of mere physical pleasure in the cooling breeze, joined with simple delight in the common green and blue of nature. But the matter of this experience is pregnant with the singular force of the spirit which has taken possession of it –the spirit which feels the breeze to be 'half-conscious of the joy it brings'.

The experience is not simply of the poet's own awareness of receiving pleasure; it is also of the breeze's awareness of giving pleasure.

Is this a metaphorical expression, or a piece of mere fantastic conceit? Nothing of the kind. Nor is it anything philosophical, if we use that word properly. It is not the result of any process of thought; it comes out of <u>Wordsworth's profound and immediate intuition of things</u>, and represents his habitual manner of experience when life was in any way exalted in him, whether by sensuous or emotional or intellectual occasions. The manner of his mind's instantaneous response to events was certainly very complex; but it was intrinsically complex, not elaborated by subsequent reflection or introspective examination. These opening lines, by a fine stroke of art, prepare us for what is to follow: the revelation of the growth of that mind whose habit it became thus intuitively to experience its relationship with the world it lived in; of that poetic personality which thus *felt* its kinship with the things it knew—a kinship that went much deeper than the mere knowing of them or the ability to know them—and which could proclaim not merely 'how exquisitely the individual Mind is fitted to the external World', but 'how exquisitely, too, the external World is fitted to the Mind'.

Out of this central habit of experience, this sense of kinship between the nature of the man and the nature of his world, speaks the poet to whom 'the meanest flower that blows can give Thoughts that do often lie too deep for tears'; whose faith it was—literally and exactly his *faith*—'that every flower Enjoys the air it breathes'; to whom it was pure truth, not merely a verbal flourish, that 'the sky rejoices in the morning's birth'; whose consolation for Toussaint l'Ouverture was his perfect confidence in the common purpose of mind and nature, instinctively joining them together in a truly sublime assumption:

> Thou hast left behind
> Powers that will work for thee; air, earth, and skies;
> There's not a breathing of the common wind
> That will forget thee; thou hast great allies;
> Thy friends are exultations, agonies,
> And love, and man's unconquerable mind.

and who, in an equal sublimity of idea, also dared to give (though he regrettably toned it down afterwards) the counterpart of this optimistic sense of man's community with nature when, apostrophizing the Supreme Being whose presence to him was everywhere, he declared:

> But thy most dreaded instrument
> In working out a pure intent

Is Man—arrayed for mutual slaughter,
—Yea, Carnage is thy daughter.

That, ever since it was first written, has been shocking to weak minds; it would surely be much more shocking to suppose that Carnage could be anybody else's daughter. The passage, it is true, is transitional; it belongs to the time when orthodox theology was taking the place of that peculiar habit of experience which made what we may distinctively call the Wordsworthian mind. But the habit was still strong enough to continue into his orthodoxy the somewhat startling tone of his pantheism, as it is often called.

I do not mean to suggest that Wordsworth's mode of experiencing nature was something new in itself. That it certainly was not. He had, for example, a most notable predecessor in the poet he specially loved, Virgil. And perhaps it is not extravagant to see in the first words of the *Georgics*, as in the opening lines of *The Prelude*, the key to the poet's intention—

Quid faciat *laetas* segetes.

The happy harvests! To Virgil, they really were, or should be, happy, and not merely in so far as they would make the farmer happy. With Wordsworth, however, the thing is the degree and the completeness with which this kind of experience inspires his

ou do not have to read him carefully in

tect it; it is everywhere in him—until the

ne.

the poet who uttered that rapturous exclamation with which *The Prelude* opens had already wholly achieved the state of mind the poem is to describe and analyse so wonderfully while narrating the history of its growth. As he walkt out from Bristol to Racedown, now at last feeling himself not only free but fit to begin his life-work, he lookt forward to days measured by 'matins and vespers of harmonious verse'; and during those two years at Racedown and Alfoxden, in company with Dorothy and Coleridge, after much struggle and doubt and debate, the form his life-work was to take at last defined itself, though somewhat loosely. He called it a philosophical poem, but it was not to be strictly that, as he himself admitted. It was to be a grandly designed and elaborated work 'containing Views of Man, Nature and Society . . . the sensations and opinions of a poet living in retirement'; in other words, a comprehensive and direct expression of the poet's own experience of the world. Exactly how it was to be carried out remained to a considerable degree uncertain; and the project eventually broke down, though it was of such a kind that its impulse and much of its proposed material could be diverted into other forms.

Meanwhile, the first thing to do was to show what
manner of mind it was that was putting itself forth
in these experiences; otherwise their nature and
significance could not be understood. This was what
Wordsworth undertook in *The Prelude.* In a narrative full of varied and often strangely exciting incident, charged with marvellous power of delineating
the aspect of things and of making this deeply expressive of the spirit that is in them, and with no less
marvellous power of putting into language the inmost and subtlest motions of the mind; with a style
that scarcely ever fails from start to finish perfectly
to adapt itself to the needs of the moment, from the
mock-heroic of

>   And at the Hoop alighted, famous Inn . . .

to the apocalyptic vision in and through nature of

>   The types and symbols of Eternity . . .

the poem shows us the growth of that central habit
of experience which made Wordsworth the poet he
was—its unconscious beginning in childhood, the
deepening, widening, and enriching of it through
boyhood and youth, and its full maturity and secure
assurance in the man conscious of

>   absolute power
>   And clearest insight, amplitude of mind
>   And Reason in her most exalted mood.

It is by no means the history of a mind merely *receiving* from nature continually increasing wealth; it is something far more subtle and remarkable than that, and it can but be crudely summarized. It is the history of a process in which the mind is 'creator and receiver both'. As soon as this mind begins to receive the impression of nature, it receives also the sense that nature means more than the immediate impression it makes; and the sense which nature gives of its own transcendent meaning increases until this evokes the mind's power to read that meaning. This power is Imagination—so called, as Wordsworth admits, 'by sad incompetence of human speech'. However it is called, it is the major power in his life; the power not only to understand that every impression nature gives is a symbol, but also to hold all these symbols intelligibly together (like the syllables or letters of language) and to read them as one continuous whole of meaning. The mind is the creator of the meaning it reads in nature; but the mind's power to create this meaning in nature has been given by nature itself. And this meaning is Wordsworth's profound intuition of the Divine community of being, the intuition which forms the central habit of all his mature experience. It is not only an intuition of community in all the varieties of nature, which can co-exist, as he often insists, with the most vivid sense of their differences, it is also an intuition of community between mind and nature so complete that he can declare, 'not in a mystical and idle sense, But in the words of Reason deeply weighed', that 'each most obvious and particular thought ... Hath no beginning'. The mind's thought, like nature's processes, has no beginning as it has no end, because the mind like nature belongs to the infinitude of things.

This habit of experience which *The Prelude* so grandly and delicately portrays, this perfection of relationship between the poet and his world, what is it but the very essence of that poetic personality we always try to know in the work of a poet? In Wordsworth, our knowledge of it is absolute; throughout his great period, all his poetry is one kind of expression or another of the poetic personality expounded in *The Prelude*. We do not have to infer its intention; we are in the unusual position of *knowing* what it is. And this poetic personality, with its habitual style of experience, is as much a poetic creation, a work of art, as the verbal technique which communicates it. It is the work of the *Muse*, as Wordsworth calls it: the spirit of collaboration between mind and nature; and it is itself the presiding creative harmony which can shape all the poet's particular experiences.

This, then, is Wordsworth's subject, this creative

harmony. Often, when we try to make out in a poet's work what I have called his poetic personality, his main theme or motive, we allow ourselves to speak in general terms—and sometimes vaguely enough—of his subject. We might say that Milton's subject is man's temptation and redemption, that Dante's is the justice of divine love disposing all things. If we speak so of Wordsworth we must say that his subject is poetic experience itself. By the expression of this, his art is inspired; by this intention it must be judged. With such a subject the accusation of egoism is to be expected. But Wordsworth's egoism is never egoism asserted as such; it is but the necessary *locus* of poetic experience. His poetry does not give us his personality simply because it was his own, but because of that harmony of mind and nature which his personality had become. In all poetry, the subject, whatever it may be, carries with it something of the poet's peculiar sense of relationship between himself and his world. As a rule, we can feel unmistakably that this personality does inform the subject, though exactly how and in what degree we cannot always be certain. In Wordsworth this active relationship does not so much inform his subject, it *is* his subject; he has no other.

He does not communicate this shaping harmony as something rare and privileged, but as a state of life into which everyone may enter. It is true he particularly insisted on the importance of this vital harmony to the poet. 'The perception of harmony', he said, 'lies in the very essence of the poet's nature'; and if it were there the poet need but trust to his feelings, 'and'—as he once told a young man—'your poem will take its shape and proportions as a tree does from the vital principle that actuates it'. For the world at large, perhaps he would not have admitted that the spirit of what he had to give was simply poetic experience itself. But essentially that is what it was; and as he gave it forth, it could become 'joy in widest commonalty spread'. This, in John Stuart Mill's famous words, is 'what would be the perennial sources of happiness when all the greater evils of life shall have been removed'. We cannot all be Wordsworths and achieve on our own account this deep experience of harmonious relationship with the world; but we can possess it as he communicates it, in a hundred different forms and manners. How he communicates it we must go on now to consider.

III. CONSTRUCTION

THE Wordsworth who, in 1795, took possession of Racedown with his sister Dorothy, and in 1797 migrated thence to Alfoxden, had already commenced poet in earnest. During those years his poetic impulse was urged, both by Dorothy's quietly encouraging companionship and by the electrifying friendship of Coleridge, their neighbour at Nether Stowey, to form in him an ambition far beyond anything he had so far done or contemplated. Nether Stowey and Alfoxden are chiefly associated in literary history with the composition of *Lyrical Ballads*. If Wordsworth at that time had been told this would be so, I think he would have been a good deal surprised. *Lyrical Ballads* had, indeed, a quite casual and light-hearted origin; the book developed out of a scheme undertaken on the spur of the moment to pay the expenses of a walking tour. True, the two poets entered into the project not only with zest but with zeal. It gave them the chance of trying out several of the poetic theories and ideals which they had been vehemently debating in those vivid and wonderful days. It is true, too, that in *The Ancient Mariner* and *Tintern Abbey* each poet contributed to

the collection one of the most magnificent achievements of his whole career, or in English poetry; of
which, in the reviews, the first was almost everywhere abused, the other ignored. But the intention
of the book was essentially experimental. Ostensibly
a manifesto of the poetic revolution, sent out with
a suitably provocative 'advertisement', it was designed to ascertain how much the public would
stand. In the fuss which was stirred up it assumed an
importance which Wordsworth himself accepted and
endorsed by writing the famous Preface to the
second edition; an importance, of course, which
turned out to be very far from adventitious. *Lyrical
Ballads*, we all agree, is a landmark in the history
of English literature, as the Preface of 1800 is in the
development of critical theory. But in those Alfoxden
days, to Wordsworth himself its composition must
have been, compared with something else that was
going on in his mind, of quite secondary importance.

For this was the broad designing, and even to
some extent the composition, of the great work
which was to be the main effort of his life as a poet,
which was to be in his career what *The Canterbury
Tales*, *The Faerie Queene*, *Paradise Lost* had been in
Chaucer's and Spenser's and Milton's. And it was
to be something absolutely his own; no poet ever
promised himself a *magnum opus* that seemed more

entirely in accordance with his own consciousness of his peculiar genius. His enthusiastic intention was to compose a reflective poem on a very large scale; and the project, as he conceived it, was one to which he might well have been content to devote a great part of his life; as, in effect, he actually did, but with some very remarkable and significant modification. It did not turn out to be so exactly suited to his genius as it had seemed, and this is a fact which considerably illuminates the nature of his genius. If this, from one point of view, may be regarded as failure, from another it gives a clear indication of the very unusual quality of his poetic impulse, the quality which makes its success so unusually valuable.

A great poem is not great simply because there is a great deal of it, or because of the strength of its motive or the force of its technique. All these may be taken for granted. In the Wordsworth of the Alfoxden days, there was little doubt but that all requirements as to strength and force would be satisfied. *Lyrical Ballads* were already proving his singular power of diction; and as for his inspiration, other poets may have had more spacious and more splendid, but none ever had richer or deeper experiences than he had known, and might expect to know. *The Prelude* is sufficient witness both to what he had known, in its history of his enchanted boyhood and inspired youth, and to what he might expect to know, in its portrait of the personality, the experiencing mind, that had developed. But something else, besides command of language and fullness of matter, must go to the making of a great poem: a power of great imaginative construction. Structural imagination there must be in any art that can truly be called great.

Wordsworth had such an imagination. The proof is, that he vividly and quite distinctly visualized the structure of his projected great poem in his mere conception of it, long before anything like achievement had been attained. He could see the whole mass and shape of it, although, in fact, its complete achievement never was to be attained. As is well known, he saw its imaginary structure in the likeness of a Gothic church, to which *The Prelude* was to stand as magnificent ante-chapel. So positive and assured was his vision of the form of his great poem that he could associate with it his minor poems as well, as being all parts of the one grand inclusive purpose of his life, proceeding from the same general inspiration; grouping them round the main structure as, in his own words, 'the little cells, oratories and sepulchral recesses' which might belong to such an edifice.

This was no evanescent vision; it was in these terms that he wrote of his still unfinished poem sixteen years after its first conception, in the preface to *The Excursion* (1814). The construction, the great design of the poem was as inherent in its inspiration as the matter it was to express. In the collected edition of his poems which in 1815 followed *The Excursion* he arranged the contents so that his readers might perceive, as he himself could, how his minor poems disposed themselves in vital connexion with and, as he says, in 'subordination' to the main work of his life, the visionary structure of which still possessed his imagination. That work, however, was never carried out. How deep Wordsworth's disappointment must have been in the failure of his ambition we can only surmise. Long after *The Excursion* was published we find him still vainly trying to resume the vast project of his youth, too long postponed. In 1830, Dorothy tells the Lambs how she and Mary keep 'pressing upon him the necessity of applying to his great work, and this he feels, resolves to do it, and again resolution fails. And now', Dorothy sadly concludes, 'I almost fear habitually that it will ever be so.'

Certainly his readers, even the most fervent of them, could scarcely fail to be disappointed when they found that the poet's grand design was represented by *The Excursion*, the only portion of the *magnum opus* published during his lifetime. We are better off nowadays, for we have the 'ante-chapel', *The Prelude*. Critics still sometimes speak as if *The Excursion* were the 'church' to which the splendid ante-chapel leads us. This is unfair, and careless. *The Excursion*, as Wordsworth thought it important to inform his readers, was but one-third of the intended edifice; and, judging by the only fragment we have of the rest, was deliberately meant to be less imposing in its architecture. For he was not pleasing himself with an airy, irresponsible vision when he contemplated the imaginative structure of his poem in the likeness of a Gothic church. The whole thing had been broadly but solidly, and indeed intellectually planned, as any great poem must be. The poem, he says, was 'the result of the investigation which gave rise' to his autobiography in *The Prelude*; his self-examination had convinced him that the subject of his *magnum opus* was to be found within his own mind. Unlike Milton and Virgil, and perhaps most authors of poems which the world calls great, Wordsworth had no need to look round for a subject suited to his ambition and genius; such a subject was immediately provided by the very nature of his own experience. Accordingly, the introductory autobiography of what he calls the preparatory poem (for *The Prelude* was left unnamed by him) was to lead on to the main body of the work, to be called

The Recluse, which would be in three parts, the first and third consisting chiefly of 'meditations in the Author's own person'. Intermediate between these would stand *The Excursion*, intended, both by its style and its substance, to provide a certain contrast with the other two parts, introducing by means of studies in personality and characteristic narratives and conversations some sort of dramatic interest and an easier tone, as relief from the poet's own lofty meditation and abstruse reflection. In fact, just as the preparatory poem is now rightly called *The Prelude* to the whole work, *The Excursion* might well be called an *interlude* in it. Thus, if we could have known *The Excursion* in the context which Wordsworth's structural imagination had designed for it, it would perhaps have gained by its situation as much as, in the structure of a church, a nave of somewhat lower architectural pretensions might gain from standing between a superb west end and a glorious choir. However, as things turned out, no one but Wordsworth himself was to know the whole intended design; though how superb the west end might have been we may guess from the first book of *The Recluse*, Part I, which is all that was achieved of the rest of the poem. What the glorious choir would have been like we have no notion. Still, we have *The Prelude*, which can assuredly stand by it self; and, so standing, must be judged one of the greatest poems in modern literature. Yet even that might gain if we could see it *placed* as its author saw it; not merely, as we must now take it, the 'prelude' in a quite general sense to the whole miscellany of his poetry, but an integral part of a single vast design, standing in exact spiritual and formal relationship with the complex unity of the grand edifice he had imagined.

Why was it, then, that Wordsworth never completed his great poem? What prevented him from carrying out the design he had so confidently formed? Not lack of industry, certainly; and it may be that much of the substance he had in mind for *The Recluse* went into other work, though the dispersal of it can hardly now be traceable. Even so, why did he abandon his original *design*? What was the cause of this failure? For failure it must be reckoned judged by his own ambition. His biography gives us no certain answer to these questions, but perhaps an answer is not difficult to guess. In one sense, the apparent failure may have been real gain. If in the original ambition there was some aesthetic mistake deeply concealed, which only practical experiment could bring out, the very abandonment of the project would testify to his aesthetic conscience; a less ambitious use of his material might be, poetically, a better use of it. I believe there was such a mistake, concealed there because he had not himself realized how original his ambition was; and I believe he abandoned his great intention because the more he worked it out towards actual execution the more obtrusive the mistake became and the more obvious that it was not of a kind which dogged determination could overcome.

What was this mistake? There is, at any rate, no doubt what it was not. The author of *The Prelude*, that splendid piece of sustained forthright imaginative structure (in most difficult substance), was assuredly not mistaken in his estimate of his own constructional ability. Equally sustained, and equally forthright and without intricate involution, is the structure of *The Excursion*, though at a somewhat lower elevation. Could not the other two parts have been done in the same way? Undoubtedly; indeed, they could not have been done in any other way. 'Meditations in the Author's own person' would not allow of any kind of artistic structure except that of direct narration of their sequence. How admirable Wordsworth's straightforward narrative could be, in giving us the deeply connected succession of events and of states of mind, *The Prelude* is enough to remind us; the things narrated there are anything but simple, but the narrative itself is as simply and plainly ordered as it could well be. Only a remarkable command of narrative art could make of such subtle and complex matter a lucid and perfectly connected story. But if all four parts of the poem had been executed in this style of straightforward narration, that would scarcely have realized Wordsworth's imaginative vision of the poem as a whole, and could hardly have given him his 'Gothic church' —his conception of all four parts uniting together in one mass of singly designed poetic architecture. The parts would merely have been continuous, one after another, each repeating its predecessor's style of structure. What was needed was that they should be not merely successive, but in their succession organized together as structure into one great composite edifice. His *magnum opus* could only have been achieved as he had imagined it, if he could have employed some such intricate complexity of structure as that of the *Iliad* or the *Aeneid* or *Paradise Lost*; and the matter to which his genius was committed would not bear such elaborate organization as Homer's and Virgil's and Milton's matter made possible.

Yet his mistake was natural, perhaps inevitable. In one sense he could regard himself as the successor of the three poets I have just mentioned. Milton had turned the epic strain from external prowess to

> the better fortitude
> Of patience and heroick martyrdom . . .

and, by diverting it from physical battle and havoc
to the warfare in mind and spirit, found

> argument
> Not less but more heroick than the wrath
> Of stern Achilles on his foe pursued
> Twice fugitive about Troy wall; or rage
> Of Turnus for Lavinia disespoused.

And in this he was carrying on Virgil's development
of the heroic theme from Homer; from the outer to
the inner life, from Achilles the objective to Aeneas
the subjective hero. Wordsworth continued this process still farther, in his theme of a mind heroically
facing the enigma of itself and its world, and resolutely confiding in its instinctive sense of their ultimate harmony. Surely he had but as resolutely to
confide in his theme, and to give to it (as his prede-
cessors had given to theirs) perfectly sincere expression, to achieve a poem—I am speaking now of
his whole project—which would continue the great
series?

But—'the moving accident is not my trade'; so
he himself was to declare. He had no such *story* to
tell as Homer and Virgil and Milton had. His
subject was the nature and reality of poetic experience itself, not the subjects that may be animated

by poetic experience. The mind, 'the insatiable mind', and its mysterious commerce with the world —that was his theme; and it must be given out directly, not by implication. Few indeed are the poems in which he uses history or legend or myth; and (in the time of his greatness) it is always as a special device to emphasize by contrast his real subject—the inmost working of the mind, or its deep community with nature. The capital instance is *Hart-leap Well*, where he shows how admirably he could tell a romantic story when he chose. But he only tells of that glorious day, and the triumph of Sir Walter's hunting, for the sake of his own sense of the event:

> This Beast not unobserved by Nature fell;
> His death was mourned by sympathy divine.

Note the extraordinary effect, in this context, of the words 'not unobserved' and 'sympathy'. Wordsworth's feelings were not simply his own; in them, nature's universal spirit expressed itself, and that was their importance for him. The poem, with its theme and counter-theme, is a wonderful instance of what a great poetic artist can do by sheer *composition*. So too in *The Feast at Brougham Castle*, the poet recaptures the splendour and excitement of a great historical moment only to bring out by contrast with

this the inner greatness of the hero's mind, a mind
that had known

> The silence that is in the starry sky,
> The sleep that is among the lonely hills.

And so it is with *The White Doe of Rylstone* and *Dion*.
Even in *Laodamia*, the most 'objective' story of all
his poems, it was not the story itself, but the moral
he saw in it, that inspired him; though a definitely
ethical moral is not very usual with him, and his
sense of the significance of things could seldom be
formulated in that way.

These are only the apparent exceptions that emphasize the general rule. In the main body of his
work Wordsworth not only could but must dispense
with the traditional topics of poetry. His heroic
theme was not of a kind that would tolerate the inter-
vention of legendary or historical substance; even
imaginary substance was for the most part no good
to him. 'Paradise, and groves Elysian, Fortunate
Fields'—not only all such dreams of the ideal world
as these must he reject, but even the kind of poetic
imagination they represent:

> For the discerning intellect of Man,
> When wedded to this goodly universe
> In love and holy passion, shall find these
> A simple produce of the common day . . .

Here 'these' means the *essence* of these, their poetic

force as imaginative symbols. The experience he had to express was in itself that essence, that poetic force; and only as itself could he express it, whatever mode his experience might take of recalling or confiding in or (at some rare height of actual passion) entering into the mystical union of the individual mind and the divine universe. Hence it is that he has no mythology. In other poets, inspiration might create an embodiment for itself in the figure and story of Satan, or of Faust, or of Prometheus; and it is in such embodiment that the grand achievements of complex imaginative structure can be attained. But no such transfiguration or mediation was possible for Wordsworth; his inspiration was such that it could not endure anything but its own direct and immediate power over the poet's language. With him, what demanded expression was the essence of poetic experience itself, not the imaginative form which, in most poets, poetic experience instinctively takes. How, indeed, can Wordsworth's experience take even such imaginative form as the Red Cross Knight or Endymion, the Witch of Atlas, or Comus? What mythological symbolism could contain it, what figures of allegory or superstition? For him, imagination was the power to combine phenomena into a glorious language intelligible to the spirit, and thereby to read human experience as an apocalypse of divine reality, rather than the power to translate experience into significant mythology or legend. However significant these might be, they could never be significant enough for him!

> For I must tread on shadowy ground, must sink
> Deep—and, aloft ascending, breathe in worlds
> To which the heaven of heavens is but a veil.
> All strength—all terror, single or in bands,
> That ever was put forth in personal form—
> Jehovah—with his thunder, and the choir
> Of shouting Angels, and the empyreal thrones—
> I pass them unalarmed. Not Chaos, not
> The darkest pit of lowest Erebus,
> Nor aught of blinder vacancy, scooped out
> By help of dreams—can breed such fear and awe
> As fall upon us often when we look
> Into our Minds, into the Mind of Man—
> My haunt, and the main region of my song.

But if Wordsworth was necessarily debarred, by the very nature of his matter, from the highest triumphs of imaginative construction, and if the consequence was that he found it impossible to carry out his grand design, we need not regret the inevitable. No poet can have all the virtues; it is idle criticism to fasten on what he has not, unless this can illustrate what he has. We have seen that Wordsworth's failure to achieve anything like Homeric or Miltonic structure is not simply a defect in him; it was the inevitable consequence of certain positive qualities, themselves of extraordinary value. We shall do best to regard *The Prelude* as, artistically, a quite independent and self-sufficient work, a highly individual kind of epic, which tells how, in the modern consciousness of things, the mind can come to terms with the world it lives in; though the poem will always deserve the title Mrs. Wordsworth gave it, as the unique means of understanding the inspiration of Wordsworth's poetry as a whole. Taken as an independent work, its straightforward construction is absolutely right for the kind of poem it is. That is true, too, as I said, of *The Excursion*; but *The Excursion* will always suffer by comparison with *The Prelude* as regards its structure, because, being of a much less daring span, it repeats the method of the earlier poem at a lower tension and with nothing like so fine a poise. The structure of *The Prelude*, though it could not have the elaborately involved symmetry of the *Iliad* or *Paradise Lost*, not only satisfies us by the forthright simplicity of its design; the lines of its design have in themselves a singularly expressive quality.

To compensate for the kind of imaginative structure he must renounce—the complex structure made possible by creating a mythology—Wordsworth, by virtue of his peculiar inspiration, had in a very remarkable degree a faculty of quite a different kind, entirely relevant to the work he had to do, and itself of great constructive power. This was his faculty of *psychological imagination*. We can see it at work in *The Prelude*; but in some other poems it can be seen even more distinctly, because their effect relies on it more. Indeed, it may be said that in Wordsworth psychology took the place and performed the function of mythology.   Most poets, certainly, have something of this faculty, but commonly it is embodied in, and subordinate to, their mythological imagination. Wordsworth, however, is one of the poets of whom that cannot be said; and moreover his psychological imagination was of a very unusual kind. In most poets, psychology means *character drawing*. It meant that in Wordsworth, but a good deal more than that; how much more, we get a pretty clear indication, right at the beginning of his career, in *The Borderers*. This piece is often reckoned one of Wordsworth's failures; so it is in many respects. But we do not have to read it very carefully to see that it is full of extraordinarily good things.

Ostensibly, it is a drama; but it was not intended for the theatre. It was written on the Elizabethan model, which Wordsworth (as was usual at that time) enthusiastically admired and completely misunderstood, having no knowledge of the conditions imposed by the Elizabethan stage. Hence it is gravely deficient in dramatic structure even as a play meant only to be read. It must be taken as a poem heedlessly thrown into such semblance of drama as may be given by dialogue. On the whole, it is not a good poem. The story is poor, and it is poorly told. But it has some wonderful moments of diction and imagery; and it has the character of Oswald, and the strange psychological siege he laid to his intended victim Marmaduke. On this character, so shocking to conventional views of human motives, Wordsworth, when he composed the play, wrote an essay defending his portraiture of so peculiar a species of villainy. It has only recently been discovered, and it is a precious document for the history of Wordsworth's mind. It is, besides, a quite masterly little treatise on abnormal psychology, showing (in so young a man) an astonishing certainty and depth of insight into the hidden springs of conduct; and it is a perfect justification on philosophical grounds of Wordsworth's conception of Oswald's singular character. However, we do not need its assistance to understand the character as the play presents it.

In his old age, the poet, alluding to this essay, told Miss Fenwick that Oswald's portrait resulted from his study 'of that constitution and those tendencies of human nature which make the apparently motive-

less actions of bad men intelligible to careful observers'. He had had plenty of material for that study
in 'what I had observed of transition in character
and the reflections I had been led to make during the
time I was a witness of the changes through which
the French Revolution passed'. Oswald, then, like
some of the leaders of the Revolution whom Wordsworth came to condemn, was not originally a villain.
He became one by the action of events on his peculiar
constitution which resulted in his claiming for himself a purely rational freedom in conduct and in moral
judgement. Now this is very like what Godwin
claimed for everyone in *Political Justice*; and it has
been supposed that Oswald was meant as a caricature
of Godwinian ethics, and thus represents Wordsworth's bitter reaction against a system which for
a while he had allowed to gain complete ascendancy
over him. But it is certain that neither observation
of revolutionary degeneration nor reaction against
Godwin will account for Oswald. Both supplied, no
doubt, very strong suggestions; but for the picture
of the man as a whole and of the soul inside him one
thing only will account, and that is an extraordinary
faculty of psychological imagination. For Oswald is
not merely a study of character; he is also a study
of those elements and motions out of which character
is made. The delineation of his behaviour is such that

we can see through it into some, at any rate, of those underlying forces of which visible character is the product.

The theme of the poem is the tragic contamination of a noble mind, Marmaduke, by an evil one, Oswald; and the fascinating thing is to see how, in 'apparently motiveless' evil, depth after depth of intelligible motive is gradually revealed as the play goes on. Oswald's jealousy of his victim's moral purity and his desire to revenge himself for the benefits Marmaduke's high-mindedness had conferred upon him—these are but the surface of his motives. Underneath lies a sort of experimental curiosity: how far is it possible by cunning suggestion to *change* a person's mind? And what will the change reveal? 'This stripling's mind', he says

Is shaken till the dregs float on the surface . . .

and he goes on

We dissect
The senseless body, and why not the mind?—
These are strange sights—the mind of man, up-
turned,
Is in all natures a strange spectacle;
In some a hideous one . . .

What sort of spectacle will the upturned mind of Marmaduke yield? This is not mere scientific inquiry; there is an aesthetic satisfaction to be looked for, the satisfaction of creating a new nature. Let but the mind which he has transformed proceed to a *deed*, and it will be fixed irrevocably in what the world calls evil. The new Marmaduke shall be, Oswald exclaims,

> A shadow of myself, made by myself . . .

and he shall be grateful for being thus re-created! 'He shall know what I am now'—

> Rainbow arches,
> Highways of dreaming passion, have too long,
> Young as he is, diverted wish and hope
> From the unpretending ground we mortals tread . . .

In the sublime sanity of perfect realism, 'False shame discarded, spurious Fame despised', when sentiment and prejudice have lost their power to hinder, and the delusions of morality have vanished, he shall find what Oswald himself found long since:

> Life stretched before me smooth as some broad way
> Cleared for a monarch's progress.

For Marmaduke to arrive at Oswald's power over life, there needs but suitable guidance; for, as Marmaduke himself has come to admit:

> We all are of one blood, our veins are filled
> At the same poisonous fountain.

And when power over life is attained, what is the reward? Here we reach the farthest depth of Oswald's motive. It is something like proselytizing for a religion. The purely rational freedom he claims has come to be the right to do and to be what the world calls evil: to be evil is to suffer; and *that* is the reward! In a sort of mysticism he longs to impart, he exults in his suffering. There is a greatness in wickedness; not because it breaks the law which other men are bound by, but because it entails suffering; and by suffering a man partakes of that which transcends the common world:

> Great actions move our admiration, chiefly
> Because they carry in themselves an earnest
> That we can suffer greatly.

This is why Oswald's freedom has become a deliberate preference for what morality calls evil. It is not in what he *does* that evil magnifies a man, but in the consequence, as the finest lines in the poem declare:

> Action is transitory—a step, a blow,
> The motion of a muscle—this way or that—
> 'Tis done, and in the after-vacancy
> We wonder at ourselves like men betrayed:
> Suffering is permanent, obscure and dark,
> And shares the nature of infinity.

This sense of greatness must be its own applause. Solitude is its condition. Society by its very nature must reduce the stature of the supereminent man, as Oswald asserts in this Dantesque image:

> Join twenty tapers of unequal height
> And light them joined, and you will see the less

> How 'twill burn down the taller; and they all
> Shall prey upon the tallest.

But the man whom the world calls evil finds in his solitude his mysterious reward:

> But what is done will save you from the blank
> Of living without knowledge that you live:
> Now you are suffering.

Clearly, if Wordsworth ever did mean to caricature Godwinian ethics, his psychological imagination very far outstripped that intention.

This *mystery of evil* is what we have felt all along in the character of Oswald. It is the chief mastery in character drawing, to make us feel the secret personality behind the outward show of action and even of thought. Wordsworth does this remarkably; but he does more. His peculiar imagination brings vividly to life the profound forces which create personality itself. It is this psychological imagination of his, rather than the management of the story, which gives *The Borderers* its structure.

But by far the most remarkable example of Wordsworth's faculty of psychological imagination, and its structural power, is *Peter Bell.*[1] The story of *Peter Bell* is pure psychology from start to finish; yet it is as close, as fine, as orderly a narrative as any tale of objective events could be.

---

[1] A full discussion of this poem will be found in the Appendix.

And this was the faculty on which Wordsworth chiefly relied for all his major pieces of artistic structure. It is thus that the episodes of *The Prelude*, and the poem as a whole, are constructed; and so it is with the tale of the Ruined Cottage and whatever other portions of *The Excursion* have noticeable poetic consistency (such as the biographical vignettes in the VIth and VIIth books), as well as with *Michael* and *The Brothers*, with *Ruth*, and the poems in ballad form. It was not, indeed, the only constructive power he had, as we may see in the magnificent design of the great Ode and the exquisite shapeliness of his finest lyrics. In his sonnets he showed how strictly he could govern large matter and strong emotion to a form exactly prescribed, and those who have criticized their structure have shown considerably less understanding of what is required of a sonnet, both by tradition and by theory, than Wordsworth had. But it is especially important to insist on this power of psychological construction, because in it we may see a clear indication of the peculiar nature of his genius.

IV. DICTION

I T is said that Wordsworth has contributed more to the common stock of familiar English than any other poet except Shakespeare and Milton and perhaps Pope. I should think this must be somewhere near the truth. It is not necessarily for their resemblance to proverbial wisdom that verses break loose from their context and pass into proverbial circulation. Sententious these popular lines often are, of course:

> The paths of glory lead but to the grave . . .
> One touch of nature makes the whole world kin . . .

But, sententious or not, the main thing is that they should have plain direct force, without any ingenious complexity either of words or of imagery. It was just this sort of language, carrying, without decoration, clear, concise, and pregnant meaning, that Wordsworth was specially apt to cultivate. He can be as sententious as any one—'The Child is father of the Man'—but his contribution to the common currency of phrases does not depend on this; and just as Pope could give to popular speech such a marvel of delicate art as

> For fools rush in where angels fear to tread . . .

so Wordsworth could make the language of every day accept not only

> The still, sad music of humanity . . .

but the magical suggestion of

> The light that never was, on sea or land.

It is a consequence of his poetic ideals that Wordsworth has become so large a provider of popular phrases. This would naturally be pleasing to any poet: to him, if he could have been assured of it, it would have been specially satisfactory. For, though he was always ready to flout the taste of the Public, he nevertheless had what he himself called a 'devout' respect for the People, making a somewhat nice distinction between the Public, which he regarded as a merely local and transitory phenomenon, and 'the People philosophically characterized'. The approval of the People was the poet's true reward. Did the critics, those representatives of the Public which 'passes itself, upon the unthinking, for the People', find it an offence against taste to hitch such stuff as *Goody Blake and Harry Gill* into metre? Well, let them. To Wordsworth it was sufficient that by the use of metre he had communicated an important truth 'to many hundreds of people who would never have heard of it, had it not been narrated as a Ballad'. It would have delighted him to know, what John

Clare could have told him, that *We are Seven* was hawked through the villages as a broadsheet, and doubtless it would have seemed strong justification of his theory of poetic diction, if he had known how many of his phrases would be taken over by the speech of the People, whose judgement he held to be the final arbiter. It would prove that in his poetry he was indeed using 'the real language of men': for him, the crucial test.

But what is the *poetic* success of such language? A phrase or line may be apt for popular repetition without being necessarily therefore good as poetry. It must also be good in its context, expressive of some particular moment of mood or imagination. There is clearly no guarantee of that in the capacity to invent phrases which the People seize hold of and quote in all sorts of contexts. That is an impressive fact which tells us something of a writer's command of language; but it tells us nothing of what criticism really wants to know. Besides, there is some difficulty about this conception of 'the People philosophically characterized' as the final arbiter. It seems an idea of the People *mystically* rather than philosophically characterized. This odd echo of Rousseauism is perhaps one of the few traits of his mind that can properly be called Romantic.

The question of the value of Wordsworth's theory

of diction has been argued backwards and forwards
ever since it was first announced. There is no need
to go over it again. One or two points may, however,
be noted. It was typically the theory of hot-headed
rebellious youth, the defiant unhesitating rationaliza-
tion of confident instinct and headstrong opinion.
We do not know how far Coleridge and Wordsworth had worked it out in their Alfoxden discus-
sions. That it was mainly Wordsworth's theory
seems certain from the fact that only in his part of
Lyrical Ballads is it really exemplified. There it was
deliberately provocative; and the provocation having proved effective, Wordsworth proceeded not
merely to explain what his experiment intended and
implied, but argumentatively to glory in it and to
justify his intention by audaciously condemning
everything else. Not long afterwards he returned to
a youthful influence—the tremendous one of Milton;
and this, it is certain, deeply affected his practice and
should, one would think, have modified his theory.
But Wordsworth's mind was stubborn; he would
not retract what he had written. He added supplementary passages and discourses, partly, perhaps, to
mitigate in some respects the vigour of the original
doctrine, but partly also to give it a more ingenious
resistance against possible objection. Nevertheless,
it may be doubted whether, at any time subsequent

to 1800, the famous Preface ever did represent, with absolute accuracy, the views he really held. Certainly, very soon after it, we find him, in passages of *The Prelude*—a poem conceived, be it noted, when the ideas of the Preface had full sway with him—composing in a style which those ideas would hardly warrant; though it was a style of which Milton would have approved. Nevertheless, the whole body of his poetic doctrine—the expanded Preface with its supplements—did substantially indicate the sort of thing he wanted to effect in poetry, and, both for himself and his readers, would do something to clear away obstacles of mere unnecessary prejudice. Besides, he knew well enough that both in the original Preface and in its supplements he had said things about poetry which were profoundest truth, and had never been so nobly said before nor with such vivid understanding of their full significance. To disentangle these from the more doubtful matters with which he had involved them, and to set them in a new train of argument as lively as the old but more philosophically convincing, was a task certainly beyond his inclination and perhaps beyond his power. So he let the somewhat complex, not altogether consistent, and by no means wholly justifiable statement of his poetic doctrine stand in the form in which it had successively built itself up.

Wordsworth's emphatic dogma, that the language of poetry should be the language really spoken by men, is not altogether unqualified. It should be a *selection* of such language. That does not mean, however, that the poet is free to use such language entirely as he pleases; selection here means, apparently, no more than the elimination of what would be painful or repulsive—in accordance with Wordsworth's doctrine that poetry must always give pleasure. Moreover, there is a further qualification. The language should be the real language of men *in a state of vivid sensation*: for 'the end of poetry is to produce excitement in co-existence with an overbalance of pleasure'. Obviously, this qualification is of capital importance. When he wished to put his theory in the most challenging way, he declared that poetry was only the language of prose in metre. But still it must be the language of excitement; and thus he was able not only to allow, but to insist on, the immense value to the poet of figurative and imaginative language, of phrasing which conveys such intricacy of feelings and ideas and sensations as may occur in an excited mind. It was important, however, to distinguish this from the artificial and false poetic diction which he detested. To establish the true doctrine he must smash the idol his soul abhorred. And that was not so easy as it seemed, for just what was the abominable thing? How exactly was the false elaboration of phrases to be shown philosophically as something radically distinct from the imaginative language which was so admirable in true poetry?

There seems to have been implicit in Wordsworth's argument a very remarkable belief (closely akin to his romantic conception of the People) which, though he spoke of it as a conception philosophically characterized, he never did philosophically characterize. He often writes as though by *the real language of men* he merely meant the region in which true poetry lives, a certain range of vocabulary, a certain kind of syntax. But, looking closely, it appears that he often has something much more positive than that in his mind. He seems to have assumed that men in a state of vivid sensation (admirable phrase!) or on occasions of high excitement, were thereby moved to speak poetry automatically, not merely the language out of which poetry might be made, but language which itself was actually poetry; and that the true art of the poet was to reproduce such utterance. He will *select*, indeed: but only 'for removing what would otherwise be painful or disgusting in the passion'. False poetry, on the contrary, consists of 'modes of expression which the poets themselves had invented'. The true art of poetry will never be anything more than 'selecting from the real language of men, or, which amounts to the same thing, composing accurately in the spirit of such selection'. It is not the business of the poets to invent modes of expression, but to take them over from the real language of men, since, provided it is spoken under the all-important condition of excitement, this is not merely the material of poetry, this *is* poetry.

Such a belief is certainly not consistent with the whole of Wordsworth's exposition of his theory. But it enabled him strongly and scornfully to condemn the diction of false poetry. Such diction occurs when, instead of attending to the extraordinary things men really say on extraordinary occasions, poets make up a dialect of their own, which they deliberately render extraordinary by ingenious artifice. How far, in the first impetus of his theory, Wordsworth meant his protest to go, is not very clear; but it was much farther than is usually supposed. It was of a sweep a good deal wider, for example, than protest against the taste and diction of the eighteenth century. The process he describes as the cause of perversity and corruption in poetry evidently began a long way back in antiquity, and has been going on ever since. As he frankly admits himself, the false diction he reprobates 'is far too common in the best writers, both ancient and modern'.

How, for instance, would Shakespeare (to say nothing of Aeschylus and Pindar) stand Wordsworth's test? Indeed, when he alludes to 'a motley masquerade of tricks, quaintnesses, hieroglyphics, and enigmas', is it Shakespeare he is thinking of? Judging poetry from his point of view, it might well be; and if we grant a somewhat hostile bias, that is not a bad description of some of Shakespeare's style. However, Gray and Pope and Johnson were more useful victims. But when he came under the influence of Milton he surely should have been conscious of the dilemma. Milton's poetry, like the sounding cataract, haunted him like a passion; but in what sense was

> Disparted chaos overbuilt exclaimed . . .

or

> the fleecy star that bears
> Andromeda far off Atlantic seas . . .

or

> Chalybean temper'd steel, and frock of mail
> Adamantean Proof . . .

the real language of men, let selection and vivid sensation do all they can? Do excited persons actually talk like that? Are not these 'modes of expression which the poet himself has invented'? Wordsworth made no attempt to escape from the horns of his dilemma; instead, he padded them by writing the

Supplementary Essay, in which, though more recent reputations were severely handled, some of the great names which, one might think, would have either suffered under his test, or showed the test up, were splendidly praised. Perhaps it is only an accident that his praise of Shakespeare does not raise the question of his style, though we note that he declines to regard Shakespeare as the author of passages which he disliked: a position with which modern criticism has made us familiar.

My purpose is not to traverse Wordsworth's theory or this part of it. That has been done often enough. My point is that the theory itself, and the fact that he stuck to it when it had landed him in impossible situations, are of great importance for the understanding of his genius. He had, I said, a stubborn mind. But a stubborn mind must have something to be stubborn about. Why was he so stubborn here? It was because his theory of diction genuinely, though in some ways very imperfectly, expressed an absolute necessity of his poetic nature. It was his public engagement to use the art of poetry in severe accordance with his conscience as an artist; there is no sterner conscience than that, and Wordsworth's was the sternest of its kind. He could not simply retract his theory. He might have reconstructed it, but he had more urgent things to do. Doubtless, too, he was put off by that nervous affliction which made the *act* of writing an intolerable labour to him.

How, then, does his theory express the inmost necessity of his genius as an artist? That is not self-evident in the formula 'the real language of men', nor even in its more exact enunciation, 'a selection of the real language of men in a state of vivid sensation'. It is to be found, however, though not directly, in the connexion Wordsworth himself sets up between *the real language of men* as the diction of poetry and *humble life* as its subject. There is no necessary connexion between the two; but it is very significant that the poems which gave Wordsworth the occasion of announcing his theory should in fact have brought what at any rate professed to be the real language of men into the closest possible connexion with humble life. He says of the *Lyrical Ballads* that he wished in them to describe or relate, 'in a selection of language really used by men', such incidents and situations as (besides throwing over them 'a certain colouring of imagination') he could make interesting, 'by tracing in them, truly though not ostentatiously, the primary laws of our nature: chiefly so far as regards the manner in which we associate ideas in a state of excitement'. This is the poetic psychologist whom we have noticed; and he goes on to show—the argument here is pretty strong, a good deal stronger than the urban mind of Coleridge could appreciate—that for this psychological purpose humble and rustic life is particularly suitable. But this is the life also that speaks 'a plainer and more emphatic language'; this is the life the poetry of which, if it be in language really spoken by men, will only endure 'simple and unelaborated expressions'. That, he says, is one main reason why he chose to write of humble and rustic life.

Here, I believe, we get a most important flash of illumination into the nature of his genius and what his genius required of him. As far as diction is concerned it required 'simple and unelaborated expressions'; that is the secret of his insistence on 'the real language of men'. How fallacious that insistence could be we have seen, and much more might be said about it. But humble and rustic life gave him two opportunities which were to him invaluable: the opportunity to use his powers of psychological imagination, and the opportunity to compose his poetry in 'simple and unelaborated expressions'. He did not compose such poetry because it would be the real language of rustic life; rather he chose to write of rustic life because its real language would justify him in writing such poetry. The difference is considerable. 'The real language of men', a dangerous idea, is by no means the same thing as 'simple and

unelaborated expressions', which is quite unobjec-
tionable, so long as it yields poetry. But, attending
closely to what he says himself, it seems clear that
the latter came first with him, and gave rise to the
former. 'Simple and unelaborated expressions': that
is the phrase which tells us what his genius really
required; and that is why he so violently repudiated
the language of the poet of whom the Public made
a favourite, language charged with 'foreign splendour of his own', with 'a mechanical device of style',
with 'modes of expression which the poets themselves have invented'. In *Lyrical Ballads* he seized
on the sort of subject which would make poetry of
pure yet emphatic simplicity *natural*; that is what is
meant by the real language of men. And with such a
subject it would be natural, too, for simple language
to be, in his own words, 'alive with metaphors and
figures', which would *not* be the 'mechanical device
of style' he loathed.

But it thus comes about that Wordsworth himself
is responsible for the notion that by the real language
of men he meant the language of humble life. Coleridge had no difficulty in showing that such language
never has been and never will be adequate to the
purposes of poetry, and that Wordsworth himself,
in the very heyday of his theory, did not find it so.
That the Wordsworth of the later poems did not use

this language is self-evident. Coleridge in the Alfoxden days seems to have been in sympathy with the
general drift of Wordsworth's theory, but that,
probably, is as much as can be said. Even at that time
he admits that he was sometimes rather mystified by
what was going on in Wordsworth's mind; later he
was not only, as a philosopher, repelled by Wordsworth's reasoned statement of the theory, but appears also, as a poet, to have lost his sympathy with
the spirit of it. At any rate, by the time he has finished
with the theory in *Biographia Literaria*, there does
not seem much left that can be said for it. Yet there
is something left, and it is pretty considerable.
Wordsworth's Preface put an end, once and for all,
to that darling notion of the eighteenth century, that
there is such a thing as poetic diction *per se*. But
indeed, though the eighteenth century made this
notion specially conspicuous by the practice of its
poets as well as by the doctrine of its critics, it is a
much more venerable chimera. Ever since Aristotle,
in fact, critics and theorists have been asking, 'What
is poetic language?' How can we discriminate the
language that is by its nature suitable for poetry from
that which is not? If these questions are no longer
asked it is because Wordsworth has not so much
answered them as disposed of the necessity for asking
them. No language is in itself poetic. Language

is poetic when it is being poetically used, and any word may be so used by the right poet on the right occasion. That, put shortly, is his invaluable contribution to critical theory as regards poetic diction. In other matters he made contributions no less valuable, but with these we are not now concerned.

In this sense, then—and it was not altogether the sense he intended—Wordsworth must be allowed to have won his general case against the doctrine of an established poetic diction. Diction is poetic only in concrete specific instances, in this or that actual use of it. In poetic diction so understood, he must even be allowed to have made out his special case in favour of ordinary language. That is to say, words become poetic by being poetically used; and the words most capable of being poetically used are the common words. The general importance of this to critical theory can hardly be over-estimated; but it is of extraordinary importance in the criticism of Wordsworth. If it was a necessity of his genius to rely on simple and unelaborated expressions, that meant it was a necessity to use them so that they would be poetry.

Obviously, the richness of poetic possibility in the common words does not exclude—as Wordsworth himself showed by his practice—words and turns of language which would scarcely occur anywhere but in poetry. There will always be, to some extent, a language peculiar to poetry; but its validity must depend, of course, on its not being used as a 'mechanical device of style'. In the eighteenth century, since it was taken for granted that there should be an established poetic diction, it seemed plainly incumbent on the poets to find out what it was. They thought they had found it out; that is what they and their critics meant by the 'improvement' of poetry in their age. So remarkably did they succeed in fixing poetic style that their work securely stood in many quarters long after the nineteenth century had exploded its pretensions. (It is proper to remember, when we note the extremes to which Wordsworth allowed his exasperated argument to lead him, that the style he so detested might well seem in 1800 as firmly set as it had ever been.) But whenever the eighteenth century succeeded in its poetry it did so not because it had established an authorized poetic diction but because its poets had found some way— and they found a good many ways—of using this diction poetically; that is, of using it in precisely the same way as *low*, *mean*, or *vulgar* words may be used poetically. Moreover, even in the eighteenth-century style, just as in the style of similar ages elsewhere (France and Italy, for instance), and indeed

generally in all poetry, the staple of poetic language
is what Wordsworth said it was—the language of
common life; if you like, the *real language of men*.
This is by no means to say, the staple of poetic language is *simplicity*. You would not call it simple
when Shakespeare writes:

> The baby figure of the giant mass
> Of things to come at large;

yet every word there is a perfectly ordinary word.
The thing is, once more, that the common words
are the words which allow most scope for poetic
use.

For what do we mean when we say words are
being used *poetically*? No one has explained this
better than Wordsworth in his account in the preface to the Collective Edition of 1815 of the imaginative power that can be drawn out of language by the
art of the poet. He gives a series of progressive
degrees in the poetical power of the same word, the
word *hang*. A parrot or a monkey may be said to
hang by claws or tail: a plain statement of fact. Nothing else is meant but that the creature does simply
and literally hang. But Virgil's shepherd says his
goats *hang* on the bushy crag, and Shakespeare
makes Edgar say:

> halfway down
> Hangs one that gathers samphire, dreadful trade.

The goats do not actually and literally hang, neither does the samphire-gatherer, but both present the appearance of doing so. The sense of their situation is heightened by the idea, and, says Wordsworth, 'the mind in its activity, for its own gratification, contemplates them as hanging'. The case of the samphire-gatherer is particularly striking; for, of course, there *was* no samphire-gatherer. Edgar's purpose is to make his blinded father *think* he is standing on the brink of a cliff, and he instinctively seeks to quicken Gloucester's imaginative apprehension of his position by thus vividly mentioning the samphire-gatherer *hanging* far below his feet. Finally, in this series of instances, we have Milton:

> As when far off at sea a fleet descried
> Hangs in the clouds, by equinoctial winds
> Close sailing from Bengala . . .
>   So seemed
> Far off the flying Fiend.

This Wordsworth himself must expound:

Here is the full strength of the imagination involved in the word *hangs*, and exerted upon the whole image: First, the fleet, an aggregate of many ships, is represented as one mighty person, whose track, we know and feel, is upon the waters; but, taking advantage of its appearance to the senses, the Poet dares to represent it as *hanging in the clouds*, both for the gratification of the mind in contemplating the image itself, and in reference to the motion and appearance of the sublime object to which it is compared.

This series, then, though intended by Wordsworth to illustrate a particular power of imagination in language, is typical of what is meant in general by the poetic use of words, showing as it does a progressive increase in the richness of meaning conveyed by words. It is the business of the poet to communicate experience; not merely to say *what* this or that experience has been, nor to assert his opinion of it, but by the stimulus of words to rouse such vivid motions in the minds of his readers as may constitute in them a lively experience which will imitate his own. The more meaning he can make his words convey, the more exactly will they quicken, in the mind that can respond to them, imaginative experience of the required kind and quality, whether in complexity or subtlety or force. The difference between the language of prose and the language of poetry is not a difference of kind, but of degree—of the degree of significance conveyed. This is what Wordsworth meant when he said, quite rightly, that there is no *essential* difference. The difference lies in the *use* of the language. Poetic language is distinguished from the prosaic by being so used as to affect the mind by every power language has of doing so, and thus carrying the highest degree of possible and appropriate meaning.

Now what we commonly call the *meaning* of a word—that which, for instance, the dictionary will give us—is but the central nucleus, more or less definite, of a whole system of significances, of gradations and suggestions and associations. The art of the poet, as far as diction is concerned, is so to combine words into phrases that they will, by a sort of chemical effect on one another, liberate and, for a moment, fix vividly and accurately just those shades of meaning which, in addition to the central meaning, will provoke in his readers the right imaginative response. Whence is it that words derive this power of expansible meaning which the poet must both evoke and control? They get it from their part in the *real language of men*, from their association with the infinite variety of action and behaviour. This is what enriches them with varying possibility of gradations of force and shades of suggestion. And that is why the words which offer the poet the greatest possibility of expansion in meaning are the common words, the words ordinarily used in everyday affairs. It is these which have been most concerned in the infinite variety of experience, and round which clings in consequence the fullest and subtlest aura of changeable meaning.

That Wordsworth in this respect vindicated his theory by his practice scarcely needs to be exemplified. Anyone who knows anything of him at all, knows what wonders he could do with the most ordinary words. One of his best-known lyrics can show us with what nicety, yet with what depth and subtlety of impression, he could commit the strangest experience, the most remote from ordinary life, to perfectly ordinary words:

> A slumber did my spirit seal;
>   I had no human fears:
> She seemed a thing that could not feel
>   The touch of earthly years.
>
> No motion has she now, no force;
>   She neither hears nor sees;
> Rolled round in earth's diurnal course,
>   With rocks, and stones, and trees.

That is a rarity even among mystical experiences: yet only one word of it—*diurnal*—is at all unusual, and how exactly right here that word is, both in sound and in meaning!

These common words, of course, are also the words most notable for their plain, direct force. It is doubtless the noblest use a poet can make of words to bring out with perfect simplicity, and perfect propriety, the full strength in common words. Few indeed are the poets who have found the occasion, or

ɪad the art, to do anything like the supreme thing
Milton did with the words he gives to Samson:

> My race of glory run, and race of shame,
> And I shall shortly be with them that rest.

But Wordsworth is one of them. Thus, in the famous
Elegiac Stanzas on the picture of Peele Castle, he
ɪays, alluding to the death of his brother John, that
the feeling of my loss will ne'er be old', and adds

> This, which I know, I speak with mind serene.

What but such perfect simplicity of language could
ɪonvey such a grandeur of resignation? And what
ɪnore sublime prescription for human nature could
here be than his recommendation of

> fortitude, and patient cheer,
> And frequent sights of what is to be borne!

There are many instances of such diction in Words-
vorth; as when Michael goes day by day to the
ɪnfinished sheepfold, the building of which was to
ɪymbolize his hopes for the son whom the world
ɪorrupted,

> And never lifted up a single stone . . .

ɪr, as in a very different instance, when the moun-
ɪains haunted Wordsworth's boyhood with the sense
ɪf 'unknown modes of being', and

> . . . huge and mighty forms, that do not live
> Like living men, moved slowly through the mind
> By day, and were a trouble to my dreams.

However, Wordsworth's theory, and its practice, have something more precise than this to tell us of the nature of his genius. When he wrote the famous Preface to the *Lyrical Ballads* of 1800, he did not make so clear what poetry ought to be as what it by no means must be. It must not be a pomp of ornamental phrases, elaborated for their own sake. For what it ought to be, his instinct was so strong and deep that he could put an absolute trust in it, even though he had not perfectly rationalized it; but at least he made its tendency quite unmistakable when he interpreted the equivocal 'real language of men' as 'simple and unelaborated expressions'. This does not mean that he wished to write poetry entirely consisting of that supreme simplicity of which I have just spoken; such lines can only occur at the rarest height of emotional and imaginative experience. It does mean that his poetry must not only reject the vicious decoration of fashionable artifice, which it would do very easily; it must also willingly renounce the splendours and enchantments with which other poets might quite legitimately delight both themselves and their readers. This, as I have said before, does not imply any paucity of technique: on the contrary, his technique is extraordinarily rich in the various means of managing the power of words. But it must never even appear to be technique elaborated

for its own sake; it must always be strictly governed
by one severely overmastering purpose; it must
never disguise, however nobly, the naked essence of
his imagination. Not for him were

> Hesebon
> And Horonaim, Seon's realm, beyond
> The flowry Dale of Sibina clad with Vines . . .[1]

nor for him to tell of

> what resounds
> In Fable or Romance of Uther's Son
> Begirt with British and Armoric Knights;
> And all who since, Baptiz'd or Infidel,
> Jousted in Aspramont or Montalban,
> Damasco, or Morocco, or Trebisond,
> Or whom Biserta sent from Afric shore
> When Charlemain with all his Peerage fell
> By Fontarabbia.[2]

His sternly commanding inspiration would not per-
mit him thus to luxuriate in proper names. Yet no
one knew and loved their value better than he did,
and so far as the unremitting purpose of his art
allowed of it, he delighted to enhance the power of
language with their suggestion and their syllables.
But it was probably Virgil rather than Milton who
taught him his more sparing use of this noble device:
as, for example, the mountain flood

> Murmuring from Glaramara's inmost caves . . .

[1] *Paradise Lost,* i. 408.   [2] Ibid. 579.

or the sheep that loom in the fog 'like Greenland bears'; or when

> From under Esthwaite's splitting fields of ice
> The pent-up air, struggling to free itself,
> Gave out to meadow-grounds and hills a loud
> Protracted yelling, like the noise of wolves
> Howling in troops along the Bothnic Main.

Note, too, the expanse and majesty given by the proper names when the imagining soul is said to be

> blest in thoughts
> That are their own perfection and reward,
> Strong in herself and in beatitude
> That hides her, like the mighty flood of Nile
> Poured from his fount of Abyssinian clouds
> To fertilize the whole Egyptian plain . . .

or the magically Romantic suggestion of the cuckoo's voice

> Breaking the silence of the seas
> Among the farthest Hebrides.

Certainly we do not go to Wordsworth for poetry 'all garlanded with carven imageries'; we shall not find in him the sun 'gilding pale streams with heavenly alchemy', nor 'summer's green all girded up in sheaves, Borne on the bier with white and bristly beard'. But he can tell us of the White Doe of Rylstone with an art in which the modulations of metre and the harmonies of syllabic sound are exquisitely present:

. . . down the path through the open green,
Where is no living thing to be seen . . .
Comes gliding in with lovely gleam,
Comes gliding in serene and slow,
Soft and silent as a dream,
A solitary Doe!
White she is as lily of June,
And beauteous as the silver moon
When out of sight the clouds are driven
And she is left alone in heaven;
Or like a ship some gentle day
In sunshine sailing far away,
A glittering ship, that hath the plain
Of ocean for her own domain.

Yet in all that loveliness, which is the most wonderful line? The simplest, the most completely Wordsworthian:

And she is left alone in heaven.

If his poetry has in it no 'deep romantic chasm' haunted 'beneath a waning moon . . . By woman wailing for her demon lover', it can take us to

The rocks that muttered close upon our ears,
Black drizzling crags that spake by the way-side
As if a voice were in them . . .

These are no romantic crags. The voice that speaks in them is not the voice of superstition or the echo of fantasy. It is the very voice of nature itself. Like all the rest—

Tumult and peace, the darkness and the light—

they are

> Characters of the great Apocalypse,
> The types and symbols of Eternity . . .

There lies the point to which all discussion of Wordsworth's art inevitably leads us. Sometimes he can be astonishingly daring both with his words and his images, as though his genius were glorying in the liberty its power gives it; witness the famous invocation of childhood:

> Mighty Prophet! Seer blest!
> On whom those truths do rest,
> Which we are toiling all our lives to find,
> In darkness lost, the darkness of the grave;
> Thou over whom thy Immortality
> Broods like the Day, a Master o'er a Slave,
> A Presence which is not to be put by . . .

That was too much for Coleridge; he boggled at it like the most prosaic logic-chopper in the world. Yet for all its apparent freedom and bold complexity, how absolutely the vision commands us not merely to enjoy the imagery as itself, but thereby to feel to the very centre of Wordsworth's profound store of experience—the vision of the boy's immortality brooding over him, *a Master o'er a Slave*! Here, indeed, is language 'alive with metaphors and figures': you *see* the Master gravely contemplating his Slave.

But the vision is not called up for its own sake, to give us the delighted sense of *imagining beautifully*. The beauty of the image opens instantaneously into the heart of that which inspires it—Wordsworth's inmost intuition of *what it means to be alive*, to be a mind receiving the universe, and creating what it receives.

The temptation is very strong, when we are trying to distinguish the peculiar quality of Wordsworth's technique, to say it is never used for its own sake; I have said so myself, more than once. That is only a way of speaking; convenient enough, but equivocal, and not to be taken too literally. No technique is used for its own sake in poetry. It would not be poetic technique at all, if it had not the one perpetual purpose of expressing or communicating. What is communicated is indeed enjoyed for its own sake, and so therefore is the art of communicating it. But within the art, technique is always entirely purposive; it is always a means to an end, the end being the existence of the artist's work *in us*. All poets must, somehow or other, directly or indirectly, express that inmost core of personality, that central habit of experience, out of which their inspiration comes. With the vast majority of poets, this poetic personality is not itself their subject; it is the spirit that animates and characterizes whatever their shaping imagination may have seized hold of. They clothe their personality in the experience they delight in, in some intricate web of thought and sense and mood; and it is to communicate this that they elaborate their technique. Wordsworth's subject is that central habit of experience itself. What inspires him is the very source itself of inspiration, poetic personality in its essential energy. This must directly govern all his art. His subject could take many forms, but no disguises. His theme is always essentially the same: it is the joy on which his whole poetic life rested, his profound sense of assured relationship between himself and the world, however enigmatic that relationship might be. This joy was indeed for him the type of the status and privilege of human nature: in that conviction lay the supreme importance it had for him. But his sense of it was his own, and as his own it must be expressed.

This fundamental joy (it is no paradox to admit) could take pathetic or tragic form. But this expression of it would tolerate no mediation. Imagination in him could no more allow itself to create a world of poetic mythology, than his verbal technique could decorate itself for the sake of incidental or qualifying beauty. His instinct for a technique of 'simple and unelaborated expressions' was the command of his genius to ignore all intervening experience, and to

express nothing but the pure essence of poetic experience direct from his inmost mind:

My haunt, and the main region of my song.

Inevitably, to this purpose great sacrifices had to be
made; and the value of this purpose and of its achievement is what remains to be discussed.

V. VALUE

WORDSWORTH was fond of asserting that his poetry would be found to have considerable _moral value._ This was natural. Evidently he himself found this value in the poetry that moved him most; and he could not but believe there would be a similar virtue in his own poetry, composed as it was in such deep accordance with his strong sense of what poetry ought to be. But this is not its characteristic or most important value. Certainly he did not mean that his poetry is to be valued by something which it shares with sermons. Poetry is an affair of a kind peculiar to itself; if it can be distinguished from all other affairs, it must have a value peculiar to itself. That is what it has in the value which aesthetic judgement pronounces on it; the value 'anything may have merely by being itself. For aesthetic judgement, in everything that may come before it, looks for an immediate satisfaction—the satisfaction which any act or thought or fancy or feeling may give simply in and for itself, without having to appeal to any criterion outside itself, or having to convince us that it is real or true or good or useful. Of such a kind would be the immediate satisfaction of bringing off a skilful stroke in a game, or of successfully answering an argument, or of learning of a generous deed, or of hearing a blackbird on a spring morning, or seeing and smelling a flower, or watching a child dancing, or fancying ourselves as light-limbed as a child. To this order of judgements belongs the aesthetic judgement of poetry, of that imaginative experience which poetic language evokes in our minds, the immediate self-sufficient delight in which reaches its height in the value we call beauty.

So far, I suppose, most people would agree. But many go on from this to conclude that poetry has no connexion with morality. There is doubtless something very attractive in a doctrine of such charming simplicity. The objection to it is human nature; that fact which is an objection to so many theories of charming and attractive simplicity. Human nature does not work in the way this theory supposes; it will not live departmentally, now an aesthetic life, now a moral life. We make these convenient distinctions a little too easily; or rather, having (quite reasonably) made them for convenience, we assume them absolutely. The mere act of judging an aesthetic value has a moral effect; just as there is always some aesthetic satisfaction in making a moral judgement. But in anything which is presented for moral judgement, any aesthetic pleasure we may have in it depends on making that moral judgement; and just so in a poem, which by its very nature is offered for aesthetic judgement, the moral effect depends on making that judgement. Indeed, Shelley's argument seems to me irresistible: imagination cannot be moved at all without some quickening of the moral life. I take it this is what Wordsworth meant when he asserted the moral value of his poetry: not that he wished it to be cited before the moral judgement, and to be approved by an ethical verdict; but simply that if it be judged in the only way poetry as such can be judged—for the immediate satisfaction it gives merely by being itself—this access in the reader's aesthetic life would necessarily be associated with some enhancement of his moral life. How, indeed, could it not be so? Is it not to be expected, that the effect of a poet's art on us, however strictly as art we take it, should be to improve our moral sensibilities just as it improves our other sensibilities? 'With what eyes these poets see nature!' says Hazlitt; it is of Wordsworth he is speaking. And they make *us* see nature with their eyes; not only while we are *in* their art, but it may be everywhere, and for the rest of our lives, as Hazlitt goes on to point out. Who, after reading Wordsworth, does not feel that this poetry has 'purged his visual ray like euphrasy or rue', that there has been added to him a new faculty for seeing nature? And of this kind is the moral value he claimed for his poetry—its power of improving the moral life by quickening moral sensibilities.

Something of this should be true of all poetry, but it need not always be such that we are distinctly conscious of it. Wordsworth's assertion meant that his poetry would be found to have some noticeable kind or degree of moral effect. Surely he was right. If we accept Shelley's argument that the imaginative and the moral life are indissolubly linked, it must follow that the greater and the nobler the imaginative experience poetry gives us, the more power it will have to stir the moral life which perpetually accompanies aesthetic activity. Many poets can rouse in us more copious or more splendid imagination than Wordsworth; few poets anything so pregnant or so poignant, of such concentrated richness of significance, or from such a depth in our natures. With such an aesthetic experience there will necessarily correspond a perceptible moral effect.

Besides those poems which may have, in this large and secondary sense, a moral effect, there are others, of course, which have, distinctly and avowedly, what is called a *moral*, which make a point deliberately directed upon the moral judgement. In such poems, discrepancy between moral and artistic values may

very easily occur, and actually does occur in Wordsworth. He does not often provide his poems with
a moral; but he does sometimes, and in one instance
at least, in *Laodamia*, he does it very notably. The
instance is the more notable because the poem is
generally regarded as one of his most admirable
things, while its moral is, ethically valued, one with
which few people, I hope and suppose, would willingly agree. Yet it is perfectly true that the poem
could not present its moral with any effect at all,
if it were not a poem first of all, and to be judged as
a poem. It compels us, with severe and noble force,
imaginatively to experience the opposed powers of
passion and resignation; and it is directly out of this
imaginative experience that the moral of the poem
strikes upon our minds. Laodamia is unable to relin-
quish the passion of her love; the vision of Pro-
tesilaus, permitted to return from the grave in order
to persuade her to resignation, does but inflame her
passion the more. The power which passion has over
her is ethically judged as her weakness, and the poet
accordingly proceeds to his moral—her condemna-
tion:

> Thus, all in vain exhorted and reproved,
> She perished; and, as for a wilful crime,
> By the just Gods whom no weak pity moved,
> Was doomed to wear out her appointed time,

> Apart from happy Ghosts, that gather flowers
> Of blissful quiet 'mid unfading bowers.

Now it is obvious that, under the guise of divine justice, the poet is offering us here something which requires of us a moral judgement; and it is equally obvious that what is so offered is, to say the least, a very disputable proposition. It is greatly said, in the course of the poem, that

> the Gods approve
> The depth and not the tumult of the soul.

That is one of the grand sentences of poetic wisdom; it goes irresistibly home, both morally and artistically. We may easily accept it as equally *true*, that the Gods, as far as we can see in this world, punish weakness as sternly as they punish crime. It is also a fact that honesty is the best policy; of which it would be futile to say that it is an immoral fact, but of which we can certainly say, that it offends morality to offer it as a moral precept. Just so we may say that morality is offended when the fact that weakness is punished as a crime is made an instance of the justice of the Gods, and our moral approval thereby demanded. There will always be those who deeply admire this remarkable poem, while they nevertheless find Wordsworth's moral repulsive.

What are we to make of such an instance? It does not help us much to say that poets ought not to do such things. There have always been, and I suppose there always will be, critics who are ready to tell a poet what he ought and ought not to do. The trouble is, that he takes no notice; he just goes on doing what he wants to do. If a poet chooses to formulate, distinctly and openly, a moral to his poem, no one can stop him. But at least we can say, that he then puts himself on a level with any other professional moralist. Instead of inviting us to enjoy what he has enjoyed he invites us to argue with him about it. As an artist, he gives us what only he can give; as a moralist, he is no better off than we are. His words can command our imagination; they cannot command our moral sense. And if we reject his moral intentions on us, what happens to the art by which he has conveyed them? So far as that rejection is concerned, nothing at all. The art remains to be judged as art. When we have read *Laodamia*, we have had a great imaginative experience. Words-worth attached to this a moral, which we reject. We still possess our great imaginative experience, and we can judge it simply as that; and our aesthetic judgement will still carry that implication of moral value which we were just now considering, that quickening of our moral nature which necessarily accompanies noble imagination. And this, so far from needing to be formulated in an ethical proposi-

tion, may be actually injured if we allow it to come
before our moral judgement. We need not allow
that; it is even possible to include Wordsworth's
moral in our aesthetic judgement of the whole poem.
For this moral of his had an interesting history. In
the first version of the poem, Laodamia is *pardoned*
for her weakness; and it is *she* who is mercifully
dismissed

> to gather flowers
> Of blissful quiet 'mid unfading bowers—

instead of this being the lot of the happy ghosts from
whose company she is excluded. But Wordsworth
felt that this conclusion was too abrupt a change
from the whole tone and mood of the poem. It was
out of a regard for artistic consistency that his so
questionable appeal to moral judgement emerged.
Most critics prefer the earlier version; that, I think,
is because their moral judgement is shocked by the
proposition the final version puts to it. But this proposition is all of a piece with the rest of the poem;
and the whole composition, moral and all, may therefore be taken, as it were, dramatically. The moral
attitude may be aesthetically appreciated simply as
a moral attitude without asking ourselves whether
our moral judgement approves of it or disapproves;
just as we take at its immediate value the ethical dis-
position of a character in a play and enjoy our under-

standing of it for the pure experience of doing so. This will always be possible when the moral which a poem proposes really does connect with the logic of its art. Thus, whatever sort of claim to moral value poetry may properly make, or dubiously pretend, this cannot invalidate the purely aesthetic judgement of it, the experience of it as something good in itself without having to appeal to any ulterior criterion. Indeed, the true moral value of poetry only exists as a consequence—a necessary consequence—of its purely aesthetic judgement.

Similar conclusions will hold, if we consider another sort of value which is often claimed for Wordsworth's poetry, its philosophical value. By this is meant, no doubt, that his imaginative intuition of things had attained to a conception of the universe which might have been the result of pure metaphysical reasoning. It was never his business to formulate this conception, but I suppose it might be put something like this. In the mind of man, the whole universe exists in the convergence there of all its forces; and this is a type of every other existence. Whatever exists does so because all other existences participate in it and meet in it. This is a grand conception, which some recent philosophy, such as Dr. Whitehead's, inclines to corroborate. But, properly speaking, philosophical value could

only be claimed for Wordsworth's poetry if it presented this conception as a reasoned proposition;
which of course it does not. When Wordsworth
proclaims

> How exquisitely the individual Mind
> (And the progressive powers perhaps no less
> Of the whole species) to the external World
> Is fitted:—and how exquisitely, too . . .
> The external World is fitted to the Mind;
> And the creation (by no lower name
> Can it be called) which they with blended might
> Accomplish . . .

he is not inviting us to approve the result of any
ratiocination; he is inviting us to share with him the
grandeur of his experience, the experience of a mind
that has learned, by feeling and imagination and
reason all combined, to live in the unity of infinite
existence, in the *creation* (as he says) which World
and Mind blend to accomplish. He is inviting us to
enjoy this experience for its own majestic sake, that
is, to take it aesthetically. We can, however, say
that the purely aesthetic enjoyment of Wordsworth's poetry is perceptibly accompanied by a
quickening of what I may call our philosophical
sense of things, without having to invoke our philosophical or logical judgement. As with the moral
value of his poetry, this philosophical value depends
on the poetry being aesthetically judged.

But when poetry is so judged, what is to be said of the value which it has for us, apart from such moral or philosophical reverberations as may be the psychological consequence of its aesthetic value? The experiences which poetry gives us—and these include our understanding of their *expression*—are valued purely for what they are as experiences. They are not good for any *reason*; they are good simply for immediately being what they are. It follows, therefore, that no description of them can ever be true, or anything like true. They can only be known in the unique form in which they have, once and for all, achieved existence—in the poetry itself. Similarly, their value can never be told; it can only be known there where it actually occurs—once more, in the poetry itself. This is the general truth; and it follows that the peculiar value of Wordsworth's poetry can never be satisfactorily accounted for by talking about it; it can only be understood by experiencing it, that is to say by reading it oneself. Still, some broad indication of the nature of its value is perhaps possible.

We necessarily take poetry in by moments. A single phrase, a single word perhaps, is enough to make us aware of it. The usual informative or reasonable meaning of words suddenly becomes a flash of living imagination in us; as when Wordsworth, instead of saying snow *covers* the ground, says it *skins*

the ground; or when he tells us how the glittering
mist that the racing hare raises from the wet grass

> Runs with her all the way wherever she doth run.

The snow and the mist are not only images *before*
the mind; the life of the mind enters into the image
of a *skin* of snow or a mist that *runs*. We are made to
experience the image, by virtue of a single word. It
is not to my purpose now to analyse how poetic
language makes itself felt, whether by simple metaphor as in those two single words, or by more complex metaphor in phrases; as when the 'sensitive'
ash-tree stirred by the wind is said to make

> A soft eye-music of slow-waving boughs;

or by distinct simile, as when Wordsworth forces
us to *realize* the ancient Roman roads of England by
speaking of them as

> Hidden underground, like sleeping worms . . .

or by mere transparent simplicity of language,
through which the poet's experience shines into our
minds like living light:

> We feel that we are greater than we know.

However it may come about, every such moment of
poetic language is a moment of experience vivid
enough to be delighted in for its own sake; and it is
out of such moments that the further art of the poet
organizes the body and structure of his poetry.

In most poets, the art is to keep the reader's mind

continually delighted with the succession of these poetic moments, always related, of course, to the consistency and design of the whole. When we think of Shakespeare or Milton, of Spenser or Pope, of Keats or Shelley, we probably think first of the *texture* of their poetry, of the lines and phrases of which it is made; in fact, of the *moments* of poetic experience we have enjoyed in it. But it is characteristic of Wordsworth that, on the whole, he does not seek to detain his readers' minds thus. He has as fine an art as any to make our minds live, moment by moment, in the experience he means to give us; but its intention is rather to lead us directly on into the organization of these moments in some large period of experience. When we think of his poetry, though we can detach from it many splendid lines and exquisite phrases, we think first of some great organic movement of poetic experience rather than of intense and lovely moments in it. His characteristic art is to be found not in individual lines but in some such period as this:

> Loud is the Vale! the Voice is up
> With which she speaks when storms are gone,
> A mighty unison of streams!
> Of all her Voices, One!
>
> Loud is the Vale;—this inland Depth
> In peace is roaring like the Sea;

> Yon star upon the mountain-top
> Is listening quietly.

No poet, I believe, can show art more admirable than this. The repetition of 'Loud is the Vale' is a rhetorical device; but how superbly justified! The use of the word 'Voice' in this context, the almost colloquial bareness of 'the Voice is up', seize on our minds, and prepare us for great matter; and how inevitably the great phrase—'A mighty unison of streams'— follows that simplicity. Note, too, the elemental sense of a valley conveyed by the word 'Depth', and the strangely impressive co-existence of its profound peace with the *sound* of perturbation—'roaring like the Sea'. In all this, though every word commands our minds, nothing detains us; no figurative language invites our admiration, but we are led directly on into the full organization of the whole complex of experience—sight and sound and feeling, all bound together in one significance. And at the height of it, just when the whole period is complete, comes the one metaphor Wordsworth permits himself, and in the magic of its language we do most willingly linger:

> Yon star upon the mountain-top
> Is listening quietly.

But the metaphor is only verbal. The star *is* listening —that is as near as language can get to the truth.

We have entered into Wordsworth's rapt experience of that secret familiarity of all things with one another, in which everything is sensitive to everything else, and the stars in heaven *hear* the sound of the waters on earth.

We talk of the simplicity of Wordsworth's poetry. Doubtless by that we mean his deliberate refraining from the elaboration of his experience, moment by moment, into the captivating phrases and the figurative language on which our attention delights to fasten. His art is, as I say, first of all so to command our minds as to lead us into large constructions of experience. But the art whereby he achieves this massive structure is often as complex and elaborate as poetry can well be. There is a famous instance in *Resolution and Independence*:

> Beside a pool bare to the eye of heaven
> I saw a Man before me unawares:
> The oldest man he seemed that ever wore grey hairs.
>
> As a huge stone is sometimes seen to lie
> Couched on the bald top of an eminence;
> Wonder to all who do the same espy,
> By what means it could thither come, and whence;
> So that it seems a thing endued with sense:
> Like a sea-beast crawled forth, that on a shelf
> Of rock or sand reposeth, there to sun itself;
>
> Such seemed this Man, not all alive nor dead,
> Nor all asleep—in his extreme old age . . . .

There is scarcely a word here that has not a singularly commanding power; yet there is not one that delays attention on itself, not one that does not urge attention to take in the whole. But the whole is as highly organized a complication of imagery and meaning as anything in Spenser. The old man is so absolutely one with nature that he seems inanimate, like a stone; but like a stone that itself seems couched like a thing endued with sense, a monster animate but reposing. Here, most elaborately organized into one complex mass of experience, is the whole scope of that 'sentiment of being' in which Wordsworth could include all things, alive or dead, and in which dead things with living, living things with dead, could be interchangeably identified. The metaphysical depth of experience which this implies is characteristic, and the art responsible for it is very noticeable. But for the art most peculiarly characteristic of Wordsworth's genius we must go to those passages in which his language organizes in our minds an experience of a depth and complexity as extraordinary and moving as its technique is unobtrusive; in which we scarcely notice the medium of words, but seem to live in immediate community with the poet's own thrilling motions of sense and feeling.

There was a Boy: ye knew him well, ye cliffs
And islands of Winander!—many a time
At evening, when the earliest stars began
To move along the edges of the hills,
Rising or setting, would he stand alone
Beneath the trees or by the glimmering lake,
And there, with fingers interwoven, both hands
Pressed closely palm to palm, and to his mouth
Uplifted, he, as through an instrument,
Blew mimic hootings to the silent owls,
That they might answer him; and they would shout
Across the watery vale, and shout again,
Responsive to his call, with quivering peals,
And long halloos and screams, and echoes loud,
Redoubled and redoubled, concourse wild
Of jocund din; and, when a lengthened pause
Of silence came and baffled his best skill,
Then sometimes, in that silence while he hung
Listening, a gentle shock of mild surprise
Has carried far into his heart the voice
Of mountain torrents; or the visible scene
Would enter unawares into his mind,
With all its solemn imagery, its rocks,
Its woods, and that uncertain heaven, received
Into the bosom of the steady lake.

That well-known passage—it can never, surely, lose its power by repetition—is an example of Wordsworth's vivid language overwhelmed, as it were, by the vividness of the imaginative experience it provokes.

What is, of course, also characteristic of Wordsworth there is the subject. Who ever made a subject
more his own than he made nature? Compared with
him, nature in all other poets is an occasional topic.
His whole life belonged to nature, and nature to his
poetry was what it was to his Lucy, both law and
impulse. His knowledge of nature had sunk so deep
into his mind that by scarcely more than an allusion
he can call up some large impression: as he does, in
one of the quotations we have just had, when he
evokes that singularly moving experience of life
among mountains—the storm-fed torrents roaring
aloud long after the hills and valleys have resumed
their ancient peace. Better than anyone he can do the
set description of landscape on the grand scale; and,
on the other hand, his poetry is full of minute observation and fine detail—the patch of wet rock that
reflects the sunlight like a diamond, the habit of the
green linnet to sing all quivering, 'perched in
ecstasies':

> There! where the flutter of his wings
> Upon his back and body flings
> Shadows and sunny glimmerings,
>   That cover him all over.

And we must always remember, when we talk of
Wordsworth's profound sense of the unity of nature,
his perpetual delight in its infinite diversity; as he

several times tells us in *The Prelude*, it was the very
intensity of his perception of *difference* in nature that
gave power and significance to his sense of nature's
ultimate unity.

His other great subject is the phenomena of the
mind, from which proceeds what I have called his
psychological imagination; his faculty of intuitively
divining the inmost energies of mental life, and of
constructing their movement in the imagery and
language of poetry. I could have illustrated his characteristic art from *Peter Bell* and the ballads and
narrative poems just as well as from what is called
his nature poetry; his art of so using words as to
keep attention continually and vividly attracted, not
so much to dwell on momentary phrases, as to move
towards the organization of large periods of imaginative experience. But even more characteristic of him
than these two great subjects of nature and psychology is that which we may think of as resulting from
their combination, or rather, perhaps as the common
foundation of them both; that grand subject which
is so easily called pantheism, and which gains so
little from being so called; that theme of the omni-
presence of divine spirit in all the workings of nature,
and of the mind that has the miraculous power of
knowing nature. This theme, as I have said, is not
philosophy, though it cannot but stir the philosophi-

cal sense of things. It is Wordsworth's fundamental
mode of experience, and it may be typified in that
sublime moment of clairvoyance that came to him in
the Alps:

> The brook and road
> Were fellow-travellers in this gloomy strait,
> And with them did we journey several hours
> At a slow pace. The immeasurable height
> Of woods decaying, never to be decayed,
> The stationary blasts of waterfalls,
> And in the narrow rent at every turn
> Winds thwarting winds, bewildered and forlorn,
> The torrents shooting from the clear blue sky,
> The rocks that muttered close upon our ears,
> Black drizzling crags that spake by the way-side
> As if a voice were in them, the sick sight
> And giddy prospect of the raving stream,
> The unfettered clouds and region of the Heavens,
> Tumult and peace, the darkness and the light—
> Were all like workings of one mind, the features
> Of the same face, blossoms upon one tree;
> Characters of the great Apocalypse,
> The types and symbols of Eternity,
> Of first, and last, and midst, and without end.

We must remember that, with the exception of
some boyish verses, everything which Wordsworth
wrote, from *Lyrical Ballads* onwards, was written
after he had had this experience, and all the other
similar or related experiences described in *The*

Prelude; after, that is, his being had developt into the personality capable of such experiences. It is hardly too much to say that all the poetry which bears the unique value of his genius—all that common consent finds especially admirable in his work—is inspired by this central habit of experience which his personality had become. His finest poems are one form or another, or carry an implication of one kind or another, of this fundamental intuition of his—this assured harmony between his personal being and the world he knows. Let me give you a very familiar instance of the sort of thing he offers us. The daffodils which he saw dancing in the wind on the margin of Ullswater gave him not only an exquisite moment but lasting wealth:

> For oft, when on my couch I lie
> In vacant or in pensive mood,
> They flash upon that inward eye
> Which is the bliss of solitude. . . .

Coleridge thought the tone of that was pitched much too high for an experience of seeing daffodils. 'In what words', he asks, 'shall we describe the joy of retrospection, when the images and virtuous actions of a whole well-spent life, pass before that conscience which is indeed the *inward* eye; which is indeed the *bliss of solitude*?' There is some wistfulness here; but he goes on: 'Assuredly we seem to sink most abruptly, not to say burlesquely, . . . from this couplet to

> And then my heart with pleasure fills,
> And dances with the *daffodils*.'

But for Wordsworth *bliss* is not too strong a word for a vision of daffodils dancing by the edge of the lake, for an experience in which the soul enjoys the miraculous gift of sensation, and thereby enters into the being of nature, unseduced by those

> Relapses from the one interior life
> That lives in all things . . .

and feels itself an essential part of that infinite community

> In which all beings live with God, themselves
> Are God, existing in the mighty whole
> As indistinguishable as the cloudless East
> At noon is from the cloudless West, when all
> The hemisphere is one cerulean blue.

It is this constant habit of deeply harmonious experience which gives such extraordinary force to the inspiration his poetry communicates to us, whether his theme be nature in the outer world or nature in the mind of man. And in this habit of experience he lived until—something happened; and he ceased, to put it gently, to be one of the greatest of poets. As to when this happened, there is some disagreement;

most readers nowadays admit that, to the last, gleams of the old power returned to him now and then. As to what it was that happened, any theory we adopt must be capable of accounting for the occasional magnificence of his later work. But what an astonishing riddle it is, the Wordsworth of the last thirty years of his life! He continued to live in all the circumstances out of which his poetry had emerged, and he continued to compose with the same perfect confidence in himself, and with the same devotion; but it was no longer poetry that he composed, except at rare and accidental moments. Why? The explanation can only be psychological, though there is no need to look for complexes and repressions. Any explanation which brings in Annette Vallon may be safely derided; and the change in his politics after his disappointment with the French Revolution, though it doubtless had some collateral connexion with the decline of the poet in him, certainly does not account for it. It is inadequate in itself, and it does not fit chronologically. Moreover, the notion that political reaction was responsible for Wordsworth's loss of poetic power is wholly incompatible with the splendour of his patriotic poetry which was the direct product of political reaction. It seems rather that the connexion should be put the other way round, and that we ought to say that the psychological change,

which at last froze Wordsworth's poetic inspiration
at its marvellous source, contributed something to
his political alteration.

What was that psychological change? I believe it
was something quite intelligible. As I have said,
Wordsworth's sense of a unity of existence transcending our mortal understanding was not a philosophical conception but an experience in which he
actually lived. It was, in fact, a mysticism; though of
a somewhat unusual kind. There has been a good
deal of dispute about it into which I will not enter
except to say this: though Wordsworth himself repudiated (in his own words) what is 'ordinarily (but
absurdly) called Spinozistic' in it, yet it was very
near akin to what may be truly called Spinoza's
mysticism. It did not identify God with nature, any
more than with thought; though nature is God, God
is not nature. Nature and thought (if it is possible
to formulate Wordsworth's experience) are not
creatures but attributes of God, and each expresses
the eternal and infinite essence of God.

Now with most mystics, the divine reality with
which their experience unites them is a personal
god; and the result, except at certain well-known
transitional stages of the process, cannot be solitude,
but must rather be, in that ineffable companionship,
the supreme antithesis of solitude. Wordsworth's

mysticism did bring him into absolute solitude. He was sublimely but appallingly *alone* in his mystery; he, the living mind, was caught up, in the solitude of his own self-consciousness, into the impersonal infinite of being; immediately knowing, beyond all the phantasms of kinds and varieties of existence, the mystery of himself utterly alone in the divine unity. Compare his case with Dante's. The reality which Dante experienced was ineffable indeed, but it led him always towards a personality, and a personality that could be loved and adored. His mysticism burned more strongly, and more marvellously became in him the power of poetry, the longer he lived in it. It was a mysticism in which he was not alone, but unspeakably *befriended*. But to live self-conscious in a mystical experience of the Divine Being of the impersonal world, as transcendent as any mystic's experience of his personal god, is to live as unspeakably *alone*; and that, for many years, was Wordsworth's experience. As something actual and immediate, and not merely discursive or speculative, such experience is a rarity, perhaps because human nature can ill support it. The mighty spirit of Spinoza apparently could bear it. Lucretius and Nietzsche, however unlike Wordsworth we may think them, seem to have been similarly inspired. Nietzsche's mind broke under the stress of it; and the madness of

Lucretius may be more significant than the legend of it suggests. But Wordsworth, we know not how, managed to retreat. He gradually withdrew his mind from this sublime habit of experience, and finally closed his consciousness against it. While he could bear it, it had been the supreme joy of his life, a joy to the expression of which, as of the experience itself, even his poetry could but approximate. But in the end the solitude proved unendurable.

In this connexion we may note how persistently, and with what evident significance for him, the idea of solitude—of man, and especially of himself, alone with nature—haunts his poetry during all the years of his greatness. And it is very notable, too, how he himself, throughout his life, impressed all sorts of observers with his air of loneliness. Hazlitt said: 'he sees nothing but himself and the universe'. It was meant maliciously; but Hazlitt's keen-eyed malice saw the truth. Already, in 1799, Coleridge had written to Poole, with profound insight, 'dear Wordsworth appears to me to have hurtfully segregated and isolated his being. Doubtless his delights are more deep and sublime, but he has likewise more hours that prey on his flesh and blood'. The comparison is with Coleridge himself. The spiritual loneliness of his earlier years stamped itself permanently on Wordsworth's manner; he continues all his life to be described in such terms as 'inaccessible', 'constitutionally isolated', 'other men did not seem necessary to him'; and in the last year of his life Ellis Yarnall writes to Henry Reed of Philadelphia (his editor and faithful admirer): 'He seemed to me a man living as in the presence of God, by habitual recollection.'

As I read it, the crucial change in Wordsworth was a retreat from that mystical experience of the world which entailed a loneliness he could no longer support. When he cut himself off from this, he cut off the native inspiration of his poetry. This was nothing sudden or abrupt. He turned to experiences in which, after that sublime solitude, he could know community with his fellow-men; and into one of these, *patriotism*, he could so largely divert the force of his mystical experience that, concentrated in the form of his sonnets, it could maintain its poetic splendour. But when that stage of his career was past, we may take as typical the *Ecclesiastical Sonnets*. The comfort and safety of institutional religion replace, without fervour but with dignity and grave serenity, the earlier mysticism, the rapture of the solitary mind. The characteristic inspiration has gone; yet the practice of the art survives. Whenever feeling and imagination come to life again, it is there ready to sustain them and give them poetic exis-

tence; with what occasional majesty of result, let the
sonnet on King's College Chapel testify:

Tax not the royal Saint with vain expense,
With ill-matched aims the Architect who planned—
Albeit labouring for a scanty band
Of white-robed Scholars only—this immense
And glorious Work of fine intelligence!
Give all thou canst; high Heaven rejects the lore
Of nicely-calculated less or more;
So deemed the man who fashioned for the sense
These lofty pillars, spread that branching roof
Self-poised, and scooped into ten thousand cells,
Where light and shade repose, where music dwells
Lingering—and wandering on as loth to die;
Like thoughts whose very sweetness yieldeth proof
That they were born for immortality.

Peter Bell has never made its fortune with the poetry-reading public. It is evident that its author thought great things might legitimately be expected of it; but it is also evident that in fact he did not expect very much. 'No poem of mine will ever be popular', he wrote to Sir George Beaumont, warning him against the financial risk of an illustrated edition: 'The *people* would love the poem of *Peter Bell*, but the *public* (a very different thing) will never love it.' That was a somewhat metaphysical distinction which the preface to *Lyrical Ballads* had made; the *public* was his grand enemy there, and it is the public that buys 'illustrated' editions; but both public and people have on the whole, from that day to this, remained hostile or indifferent to *Peter Bell*, illustrated or not. Yet in its intention the poem is one of the most original and daring things in our literature, and in its success, one of the most remarkable.

Its primary composition belongs to the wonderful Alfoxden days of 1798; and indeed it is in some respects the crowning achievement of the tendencies in style and matter usually accepted as characteristic of that period—tendencies which *Lyrical Ballads* have made so famous. Poetically, *Peter Bell* certainly cannot compare with the *Tintern Abbey* lines; that poem anticipates a rather different Wordsworth, the poet who in the Immortality

Ode and the great passages of *The Prelude* and *The Excursion* was to continue, though with profoundly individual genius, the grand tradition of English poetry. The Wordsworth of *Peter Bell* was the defiant rebel against tradition: *in excelsis*, the innovator of *Lyrical Ballads*, who yet could make of turbulent innovation extraordinary artistic success. In *Peter Bell* Wordsworth was so far ahead of his time that the poem is still, apparently, ahead of the time today. He kept it by him unpublished for twenty years, eliminating from it what he judged might prove too shocking. If he hoped by this delay to gain a fair hearing for the poem, he was disappointed. His best admirers were disconcerted. The poem was misunderstood and derided when it was published, and has been misunderstood and derided ever since.

Now this is a little curious. There may still be some question as to Wordsworth's status as an *artist*, but I think it is right to say that nowadays it is mainly concerned with the later Wordsworth, in whom a failure of inspiration is discerned, as against the earlier, in whom an astonishing *power* of inspiration, whether we like it or not, can scarcely be disputed. His earlier work, so much of which was rejected as strange and absurd by his contemporaries, is now generally acceptable for serious consideration. But *Peter Bell* is the great exception. It is the Wordsworthian choke-pear. The notion that no one can swallow *Peter Bell* is so strong that no one tries to swallow it. And yet something, and something very admirable, of his peculiar genius is more distinctly to be found here, perhaps, than anywhere else.

I will go further; I will say it is a poem that achieves something unlike anything that was ever done before or since. And I will add that this is something of extraordinary promise for the future of poetry, and of special interest today. For one of our great words today is 'psychology'. There are very few poems whose inmost motive and meaning really and truly belong wholly to psychology. *Peter Bell* is one of them, perhaps the only one; certainly the greatest.

If this is so, how is it that *Peter Bell*, unlike the rest of the early Wordsworth, has remained on the whole under a general obloquy—an amused misprision it has had to bear from the first? Partly, I think, because it is sometimes as fatal to poems as to dogs, to give them a bad name; and *Peter Bell* has had several bad names. The first of them was bestowed by its author. *Peter Bell* was not only revolutionary in making a story wholly out of a process of psychology. Wordsworth, as I have said, was in his most defiant mood when he composed the poem; and his flouting of received notions of the 'poetic' was all too plain in its unpromising and uncompromising title. That was perfectly deliberate, of course, as the two mottoes from Shakespeare he prefixed to the poem show:

What's in a *Name?*

.   .   .

Brutus will start a Spirit as soon as Caesar!

Yes, a *Spirit* was what Wordsworth wanted to start, the Spirit of the Mind, the mysterious Power that lives, however deeply it may be concealed, in any mind whatsoever, by the mere fact of being that miracle, a *mind*.

The grossest case, the most brutish, would do; in fact, the more unlikely, the better. *Peter Bell* was the very name for Wordsworth's purpose. But the suggestion, in those uninviting syllables, of a theoretic and humourless defiance, confirmed perhaps by what one may find on casually dipping into the poem, has given it a bad name which it has never yet been able to lose; chiefly because it has also been given no less than two other bad names, by the deadliest and most mischievous of fairy godmothers, parody.

Wordsworth's was not the first *Peter Bell* to appear; a much more entertaining poem, with the same title, just forestalled it. A few days before he at long last brought out, in 1819, the immensely serious challenge of 1798, so carefully revised and so conscientiously considered during all those years, its reception was cruelly queered by John Hamilton Reynolds's wicked practical joke, the *first Peter Bell*, with a preface signed *W. W.* and an impudent motto from *A Bold Stroke for a Wife*: 'I do affirm I am the real Simon Pure.' Reynolds could not have known what Wordsworth's *Peter Bell* was about, or he would never have missed the chance its story gave him. But he surely knew something of the poem, by vague repute or garbled recital; he imitates, sometimes roughly but more often quite closely, its peculiar stanza. His main business, however, was to ridicule (pretty shrewdly, for an admirer!) Wordsworth's poetic pretensions in general; and he makes sufficiently readable farce of the Wordsworthian habit of ordering 'moral thunder from buttercups', of the famous Wordsworthian egoism, and of various

well-known natives of the Wordsworthian Parnassus.
Reynolds's Peter Bell is an old man in a graveyard:

> It is the thirty-first of March,
> A gusty evening—half past seven.

So he begins, and then:

> Beneath the ever blessed moon
> An old man o'er an old grave stares,
> You never look'd upon his fellow;
> His brow is covered with grey hairs,
> As though they were an umbrella.

Peter is poring over the gravestones of his friends and
relations, and the poet explains who he is:

> Betty Foy—*My* Betty Foy
> Is the aunt of Peter Bell;
> And credit me, as I would have you,
> Simon Lee was once his nephew,
> And his niece is Alice Fell.

Indeed, a complicated family. But they are all dead, dead
and buried, and Peter finds their graves one after
another, theirs and the rest of his friends and relations:
Harry Gill, Goody Blake, Old Matthew, Martha Ray,
Andrew Jones—even the Ancient Mariner (a 'relation'
of a kind the parodist hardly perceived—but still, for
Reynolds, apparently, in 1819, one of Wordsworth's
people); they are all here, and, after brief notoriety,
all dead.

> Patient Peter pores and proses
> On, from simple grave to grave . . .

but he has not yet found the one he is looking for. At
last he discovers it—and now he can go home in peace,

for he spells out the blessed inscription which sets him free:

> He reads: 'Here lieth W. W.
> Who never more will trouble you, trouble you':

the grave, is it, of Wordsworth's reputation? At any rate the parodist adds, pungently enough:

> The death they say was suicide.

Poor stuff, perhaps; though comic in its day. No one reads it now; but it served its turn only too well, and something of its effect remains. It created an atmosphere of ridicule in which it was hard to take the real *Peter Bell* seriously. In any case, that would not have been too easy; Wordsworth himself, unfortunately, had seen to that. Worse was to follow. Reynolds made it difficult (and the difficulty has become a sort of tradition) to discount a few accidents of oddity in manner for the sake of the whole meaning of the poem. A later parodist was at pains to misrepresent that meaning itself, and make it odious. This was Shelley in *Peter Bell the Third*, which I have no doubt is the best known of all three Peter Bells. It was not published until 1839, and thus continued in a more indignant and perhaps more damaging style the misprision and scornful rejection of Wordsworth's ill-fated experiment, after whatever fire there was in Reynolds's squib had gone out. And I believe that something, and perhaps a good deal, of Shelley's misrepresentation may still sound plausible today. *Peter Bell the Third* was written in 1819 under the influence not merely of Wordsworth's poem but of Leigh Hunt's *Examiner* review of it and Keats's review

of Reynolds's parody in the same journal. *Peter Bell*
(the real one) had alarmed all Leigh Hunt's superstitious
dread of didactic poetry; he called the poem 'a didactic
horror', supposing it to be a sort of tract inculcating the
benefits of evangelical piety among the poor. This was
a gross error in criticism; but, reinforced by news of
Reynolds's successful gibe, it set Shelley off on his
brilliant performance; for, in itself, that is certainly
what it is. *Peter Bell the Third* takes the form of a
sequel to Wordsworth's poem, satirically following up
Peter's conversion. It contains all Shelley's hatred of
religion, especially the evangelical and methodistical
kind, some of his skilfullest assaults on the many other
things he loathed, and some also of his finest and sanest
enthusiasms. It is not always very clear in its action,
but it is admirably written throughout—tense, energetic,
and biting, evidently spurred on by strong feeling.
What was that feeling? It was useless for Mary Shelley
to say 'Nothing personal to the author of *Peter Bell* is
intended'. One might almost say nothing else is intended.
The poem is simply an attack on Wordsworth; not on
the poetic doctrinaire who was so derided, but on the
Wordsworth who was, and by the uninformed still is,
so disliked—the *reactionary*, the man who turned to
comfortable orthodoxy after the noble ardours of pantheism, who turned Tory after revolutionary republi-
canism, who hardened his heart against everything
generous in his time; the Lost Leader, in fact—a figure,
as we now know, ninety per cent mythical. Shelley's
Peter Bell, the converted Peter Bell, is in fact Wordsworth himself; a caricature of the Wordsworth he so

bitterly disliked, done with admirable malice. Nothing could more effectively rouse prejudice against Wordsworth's *Peter Bell* than Shelley's *Peter Bell the Third.*

So far as *Peter Bell*, and not the character of its author, was the object of Shelley's fierce animus, the real source of all this brilliant indignation is not the poem itself, but Leigh Hunt's petulant misjudgement of it. It is true that the story of the poem begins with Peter as a bad man and ends with him as a person converted to goodness and a lively sense of religion. It is ludicrously untrue that it is what is called a pious story. The whole force of the poem lies in the psychological process by which this conversion comes about. Wordsworth indeed tells us a good deal about the *old* Peter, the wicked personality that is *undone*; not because he is a horrible example but because that is what it all starts from, that is what governs and characterizes the process Wordsworth sets going. But he tells us very little about the *new* Peter, the pious convertite; he does not seem specially interested in him, and certainly does not invite our interest. All he says is that Peter

> Forsook his crimes, renounced his folly,
> And, after ten months' melancholy,
> Became a good and honest man.

What he *is* interested in is *how* this happened. The purpose is no more pietistic or morally didactic than William James's in his great treatise, *The Varieties of Religious Experience.* And it has always been a wonder to me that James never alludes to Wordsworth's exciting version of the great topic of that famous work. Perhaps he did not realize how remarkably Wordsworth's sure imagination had anticipated his own scientific analysis of that spiritual process by which a personality may be created anew.

The thing is that Wordsworth has made *poetry* of his version. A celebrated epigram of his comes in inevitably here. 'Poetry is the breath and finer spirit of all knowledge: it is the impassioned expression which is in the countenance of all science.' Now in psychology Wordsworth certainly had the knowledge and the science, though I do not know how he had gained them except by the power of his genius. That he had them, his recently recovered essay on his own performance in *The Borderers* is enough to tell us. But *Peter Bell* is poetry not because of the psychological substance it gives us, subtle and strange and wonderfully original though that is. It is poetry because, by his diction and imagery, he so strongly conveys the spirit of this substance and the passion to which it kindled his imagination. The spirit is his intuition of the secret relationship which must exist between nature and a mind apparently impenetrable by nature; he conceives the brutish mind of Peter Bell brought by a simple train of events into such a state that nature can pierce it with fearfully and agonizingly revolutionary force. And the passion is Wordsworth's burning curiosity in the way the mind works, and his deep excitement in the *truth* of his own intense experience of imaginatively creating the history of the process by which a new soul came to Peter Bell.

If we think this is to attribute too much to nature, we do not understand Wordsworth. By the time he went to Alfoxden he was already in complete possession of that habit of experience which made him, when he had found the mode of expression which suited it, one of the supreme poets of the modern world. For many years it was his constant inspiration, and its creative energy could take many forms. What it was and how it grew we read in *The Prelude*. It presents itself in his poetry in two great aspects or faculties. First, nature is perceived as the great apocalypse of first and last and midst and without end. But where does that perception exist? In the mind—'my haunt, and the main region of my song'. And the infinite possibility in the life of the mind absorbed his imaginative observation equally with the infinite variety in the appearance of nature. Both were manifestations of one divine mystery. Too much has been made of Wordsworth's *discovery* of humanity after his youthful absorption in nature. Nature for him had never excluded man any more than nature itself was excluded when he called the mind the main region of his song. At first, indeed, man—*other men*, at least—had seemed merged in the general spectacle of nature, like his vision of the shepherd on the misty hills:

> In size a giant, stalking through thick fog,
> His sheep like Greenland bears.

But this life in nature was a continual widening and deepening of its meaning; the enchanting spectacle changed to a language that spoke divinely and intelligibly to his mind; and thence in the working of the mind of man he read the central presence of the universal being. The two faculties were profoundly a unity; he had an absolute instinctive confidence in the common purpose of mind and nature and this confidence gives to his faculty of psychological imagination not merely intensity but an extraordinary nicety and depth of intuition. He followed the workings of the mind with the scrupulous precision of a scientist, but with a poet's sense of significances that must be felt rather than thought. Coleridge complained to Hazlitt that Words-worth was not interested in 'traditional superstition'. How should he be? What meaning could the *super-natural* have for one to whom *nature* itself was divine? There can be no supernature. How should he be moved by superstitious wonder, to whom the most obvious and indubitable fact in the world had become essentially miraculous: the fact that every man can say 'I am I', and in saying so must necessarily imply the world in which '*I am*'—the standing miracle of man's mind in the midst of nature, and capable of knowing nature, and so the divine in nature?

But it is in *wonder* that the truth of poetry exists; that was one of the things *Lyrical Ballads* was to demon-strate. And the wonderful in poetry (or anywhere else) requires some compounding of the mysterious and un-fathomable with the actual and familiar; *both* are needed. So, when Coleridge and Wordsworth, in planning *Lyrical Ballads*, made their famous division of labour, Coleridge undertook to give to supernatural events the 'semblance of truth', while Wordsworth was to reveal in affairs of the common everyday world something 'anala-gous to the supernatural'; not so much, as Coleridge supposed, by investing them with the charm of nature's beauty, as by imaginative insight into the inexhaustible wonder of man's mind. The real counterpart of *The Ancient Mariner* is not Wordsworth's contributions to *Lyrical Ballads*: it is *Peter Bell*. Coleridge's method had splendidly triumphed; the corresponding triumph for Wordsworth's method was to be *Peter Bell*. Coleridge's success was poetically to realize the unbelievable. The marvellous, with him, was the impossible. Wordsworth doubtless thought he had undertaken the nobler task. He would take actual things, and show them to be marvellous in the very fact of being actual; not the marvellous so rendered as to suspend disbelief, but to *command* belief in its real possibility; the endless miracle of the mind at work, of mind and nature mysteriously corresponding. This was what he set out to do, and in great part did, in *Peter Bell*.

Analogies between the two poems are easily tabulated and do not matter much except as they show a certain kinship in poetic ambition. Both poems relate the story of a journey which goes through many vicissitudes of mood. In both a man of the people has a marvellous experience, told in ballad style and a new diction. Both end in his conversion; and in both a chief means of this is an animal. With Coleridge, characteristically enough, it is an albatross, loveliest and most romantic of creatures; with Wordsworth, and it is equally characteristic, an ass. But who thinks of the ancient Mariner's conversion? It is lost in the enchanting magic of Coleridge's poetry. In *Peter Bell*, however, the conversion—or rather the process by which it came about—is not only the whole purpose of the poem, but itself supplies the poetry. Coleridge used psychology, or at

least recognizably human behaviour, to give his magic
the 'semblance of truth'; Wordsworth's, too, was to be
a tale of wonder, but psychology was to be not only the
solid substance of it, but a substance which was itself,
inherently, 'analogous to the supernatural'.

For his purpose, in those Alfoxden days, to admit
any sort of mythology into the method of his poetry
would have been as much an artistic disloyalty as to
admit conventionally ornate diction. In the capital
instance of *Peter Bell* he felt bound, perhaps rightly,
to make this clear; but he unfortunately chose to do so
in a tone of burlesque—a tone unsuited to his genius.
This at once placed him (he was serenely unaware of any
such thing) at a distressing disadvantage compared with
Coleridge. Coleridge's purely imaginative purpose
needed very little narrative machinery to set his story
going; and how absolute it is, in its concise perfection!

> It is an ancient Mariner,
> And he stoppeth one of three.
> 'By thy long grey beard and glittering eye,
> Now wherefore stopp'st thou me?'

There is no resisting that. But Wordsworth has to
explain his unusual and difficult intention; and his prologue, with its burlesque disclaimer of supernatural
wonder and all that incredibly clumsy narrative machinery of his—the party in the garden, with the Squire
and the Vicar and little Bess and 'my good friend
Stephen Otter' (who exists simply and solely to rhyme
with Peter Bell the Potter), and the intrusion of their
unnecessary conversation into the story—how unlike
the force of the wedding guest's interruptions!

'God save thee, ancient Mariner!
From the fiends that plague thee thus!—
Why lookst thou so?'—

These very prolonged preliminaries of Wordsworth's are all too easy to resist. And doubtless this prologue, with its unhappy travesty of accepted modes of the marvellous—the praeternatural and the fantastic—has done much to fortify the common prejudice against the poem. It is enough to repel all but the most devout. Yet even here there are lines of true inestimable metal; and the stanzas that sum up the whole purport of the prologue are justly famous:

> Long have I loved what I behold,
> The night that calms, the day that cheers;
> The common growth of mother-earth
> Suffices me—her tears, her mirth,
> Her humblest mirth and tears.
>
> The dragon's wing, the magic ring,
> I shall not covet for my dower,
> If I along that lowly way
> With sympathetic heart may stray,
> And with a soul of power.
>
> These given, what more need I desire
> To stir, to soothe, or elevate?
> What nobler marvels than the mind
> May in life's daily prospect find,
> May find or there create?

What nobler marvels than the mind? And when the story does at last begin, psychology, as the stuff of a tale of wonder and a fountain of poetry, does indeed nobly justify itself and Wordsworth's professions.

I have used the word *psychology* several times; and I

have implied that I mean by it something unusual in poetry. But the word itself, in the *criticism* of poetry, is nowadays, as we all know, nothing unusual. It is, however, very seldom that it means much more than the delineation of character, even in drama, or such elaborate studies as *Mr. Sludge the Medium*: character formed and settled, though it may be elastically responding to circumstance. But character may change; and the *fact* of such a change, too, may be represented in poetry. Here again by psychology is meant as a rule something *static*; we are shown first one kind of behaviour, and then its successor, in the same personality; and we are told, perhaps, what gave the impulse to the change. We seldom see into the actual process of the change. Character, however, may be regarded as the visible equilibrium of invisible forces. Wordsworth, in *The Borderers*, had already shown a singular power of seeing through character into those elements and motions of the mind which underlie it. In *Peter Bell* he goes further, and makes poetry of a truly *dynamic* psychology: that inmost working of the mind out of which character emerges, the movement of conscious, half conscious, and quite unconscious forces which not only make but can alter character—sometimes in that complete and revolutionary manner which we call a *conversion*. In *Peter Bell* we are told the story of the process by which a secure equilibrium of character is disturbed, destroyed, and after an agony of dissolution settles again into a new and strangely different equilibrium. The psychological *process* is the thing; a process which is at once intelligible and marvellous.

We see first, and see into, the original of this natural miracle, the mean and hardy ruffian . . .

> . . . a Carl as wild and rude
> As ever hue-and-cry pursued . . .

a character exactly and nicely delineated, with some Dantesque concision of *living picture* (as, for example, the wrinkling of his forehead, half

> By thinking of his '*whens*' and '*hows*';
> And half, by knitting of his brows
> Beneath the glaring sun . . .

a personality in whom (this is important) you do not discern *courage* but instead 'a medley air Of cunning and of impudence'. Living in the midst of nature he excludes it by his brutish self-sufficiency. I will not quote the famous lines about the primrose, but rather these— typical of Wordsworth's pregnant suggestion—which indicate what nature so far has done to him:

> There was a hardness in his cheek,
> There was a hardness in his eye,
> As if the man had fixed his face,
> In many a solitary place,
> Against the wind and open sky!

Nature has markt this man, but it is because of his *opposition* to nature. He has fixt himself *against* nature.

The story begins with Peter, on a bright moonlit night, taking a path which he does not know but which promises a short cut. The path *betrays* him; it does not go as he thought it would. Now Peter is full of that crude instinctive animism that reads in the apparent hostility of things the same sort of intentional malice he knows he can exert himself; when things frustrate him he loses his temper with them. So he rages against this treacherous path; and with his emotions thus loosened the path suddenly lands him in a deserted quarry, with 'shadows of strange shape' about him. It seems to Peter that a decidedly sinister trick has been played on him. He presses on; but the effort to collect himself in order to do so confesses that the *aspect of things* has for a moment daunted him (clearly brought out in some lines Wordsworth unhappily cut out:

> What, wouldst thou daunt me, grisly den?
> Back must I, having come so far?)

But what follows? In a place of extraordinary but, so far as Peter is aware of it, *ironic* beauty, he sees a masterless ass by the riverside. His mood passes instantly into exultation—a prize! An ass to be had for the driving of it! But the ass will not obey him; there is something uncanny in its stubborn posture, looking stedfast down into the river. An ass to disobey him! He feels his familiar world is in some strange mutiny against him; and his exclamation, 'There is some plot against me laid' shows that the enemy has got home to him. But only for a moment; and that is typical of this part of the poem. The action is a see-saw of ups and downs; one moment Peter is at the height of confidence, the next all dissolved in unaccountable fear, and each apparent recovery of mastery leaves him the more at the mercy of some unexpected incident which somehow seems to carry immense insane significance.

It would take too long to go through all this: how, for instance, when the ass 'turns round his long left ear'

the conviction of *something wrong* strikes deeper—'sus-
picion ripened into dread': how Peter restores his confidence by something he *can* do—he can thrash the
beast: how the ass brays—

> But in the echo of the rocks
> Was something Peter did not like.

This part of the story, narrating, with exquisitely fatal
logic of psychological progress, the gradual under-
mining of Peter's habitual mode of consciousness, is
done in extraordinarily minute and subtie detail. Of
the penetrating nicety of Wordsworth's imagination
here, two examples must suffice. When the ass brays
a second time, it sounds more horrible than before—
'and the rocks staggered all around'. The sapling drops
from Peter's hand—'threat has he none to execute'—
and he is aware of mutiny not only in his world but in
his own mind. This vague uncomfortable sensation
expresses itself by making him *ashamed of himself*, but
in a manner still characteristic of his original personality: 'if any one should come', he says, 'they'll
think . . . I'm *helping* this poor dying brute'—the old
unregenerate Peter vainly trying to reassert himself!
Then in the river he sees the dead man, the ass's drowned
master; the mingled horror and uncertainty of his perception is indicated by Wordsworth in that phantas-
magoria of grotesque and sinister images that comes,
dreamlike, to its crazy climax with the famous 'party in
a parlour, all silent and all damned' (rejected, after
1819, for no known reason). Peter falls into a trance;
but on awakening momentarily recovers himself, and
his self-confidence—how? By recovering his staff—an

amazing stroke of imaginative genius! It is not now because he longs to assert himself in cruelty to the ass, for a new Peter is dimly emerging; but who does not know how, to take hold of an instrument of *one's own*, familiar to the handling of everyday habit, seems to reassure the sense of *one's self*?

It is the beginning of a new Peter. I can only sketch the results of Wordsworth's profoundly logical imagination. Peter draws the dead man out of the river, and is conscious of *pity* in doing so. He obeys the ass's caresses, mounts, and rides off. The ride is one long succession of spiritual agonies. The whole world seems to accuse him; the rocks 'change countenance, And look at Peter Bell'. (Note the concision and restraint in this simplicity of diction; no more need be said than that the rocks *look* at him.) And the whole world seems to pursue him too, secretly and furtively:

> But whence this faintly-rustling sound
> By which the journeying pair are chased?
> —A withered leaf is close behind,
> Light plaything for the sportive wind
> Upon that solitary waste.

This is a fearful thing to him:

> The very leaves they follow me—
> So huge hath been my wickedness!

He miserably tries to justify himself; but it is in the language of the old Peter:

> I'm not the man who could have thought
> An Ass like this was worth the stealing!

All the time the man is breaking to pieces; the *Spirits of the Mind,* those terrific forces held in the equilibrium of a personality, like the atomic forces in matter, are breaking loose. Finally, remorse (so the Spirits agonizingly make themselves felt) becomes hallucination

> Upon the rights of visual sense
> Usurping, with a prevalence
> More terrible than magic spell . . .

and he sees himself and the wretched victim of his former wickedness, there by the wayside as though physically present—dreadful confrontation! Now he is all dissolved in formless ruin; and now strikes in the new power that can *command,* and enchant into new order the meaningless disorder his being has become, like the power of a magnet over a shapeless scatter of iron filings, controlling them into shapely lines of settled pattern. It is the psalm-singing and passionate call to repentance of some methodists in their lonely worship. He has now arrived at the miserable home of the drowned man, and has to face the lamentable grief his arrival with the ass brings there. And then the new Peter, still in the torment of emergence from the old, looks up and

> sees the Ass
> Yet standing in the clear moonshine . . .

the placid, faithful animal; and the broken heart exclaims, revealing all the marvellous change he has endured, humbling himself before the beast his former wickedness had gleefully tortured: 'When shall I be as good as thou?' Could humiliation go deeper? Or into greater certainty of peace?

Well, we may make that the moral of Wordsworth's challenge if we like; he himself can scarcely be said to have done so. His challenge was that poetry can find its proper substance in the inmost working of the mind; of any mind, however unpoetic it may seem. His brave attempt and, as I think, his astonishing success, should be of peculiar interest today; for we are all psychologists nowadays. I do not find in the poetry of today anything like the courage of his determination or the felicity of his insight, joined with such subtlety of technique; but I do find a good deal of effort which might profit by study of this singular example of truly psychological poetry.

INDEX